OKINAWA

OKINAWA

LT. COL. A. J. BARKER

A Bison Book

First published in the USA for
K Mart Corporation,
Troy, Michigan 48084

Copyright © 1981 Bison Books Limited

Produced by
Bison Books Limited
4 Cromwell Place
London SW7

Library of Congress Catalog Card Number:
81-80454

ISBN 0-88365-547-0

Printed in Hong Kong

Page 1: Troops from the 5th Marines
were held up for 48 hours on this ridge,
two miles north of Naha.
Page 2–3: USS *New Mexico* bombards
Okinawa, April 1945.
Page 4–5: Transports gathered off the
coast of Okinawa, 13 April 1945.

CONTENTS

1. ISLAND HOPPING

By October 1944 the tide of war had very definitely turned against Japan, and the Americans in the Pacific were confounded by their successes. The question was not what to do next but how to do it. The US Air Force believed that bombing the home islands would bring Japan to her knees, but the US Army considered that an invasion would be necessary. The US Navy's job was virtually completed. Command of the sea had been won and sea lines of communication to the Western Pacific were secure. Naval forces could now be used to support ground and air operations.

In July, after the Battle of the Philippine Sea, Admiral Raymond A Spruance, the Commander of the US Fifth Fleet in the Central Pacific, had recommended the capture of Okinawa as the next step on the

road to Tokyo. He was overruled, as the flamboyant General MacArthur wanted to return to the Philippines and Admiral Ernest J King, Chief of Naval Operations, advocated the invasion of Taiwan. However, the US Army Chiefs of Staff claimed that for such an invasion nine more divisions than were available in the whole Pacific Theater before the fall of Germany would be required. In the event a plan proposed by Admiral Chester W Nimitz, the US Naval Commander of the Pacific Ocean Area, was ultimately accepted. Luzon in the Philippines would be liberated first by MacArthur's forces; then the Ryukyu group islands – the largest one of which was Okinawa – would be occupied by Lieutenant General Simon Bolivar Buckner's Tenth Army transported by Spruance's

Left: Fleet Admiral Ernest J King was the commander in chief of the US Fleet and the leading proponent of the United States' Pacific offensives, which often contradicted the Allied 'Europe-first' strategy.
Below left: The Combined Chiefs of Staff Committee brought together British and American top-level strategic planners.

Above: American GIs in action on Luzon, where mopping-up operations continued until September 1945.
Below: American commanders pictured at lunch. From left, General H Arnold, Admiral W Leahy, Admiral E King and General G Marshall.

Fifth Fleet. Initially MacArthur's forces were scheduled to help out in the Okinawa campaign but they were subsequently diverted to mopping-up operations in the Philippines and Borneo.

The overall plan changed slightly when it became apparent that possession of the pear-shaped, rocky island of Iwo Jima in the Volcano Islands was essential to the US advance toward Japan. Iwo Jima has an area of only eight square miles, but in Japanese hands it menaced US bombers from Saipan that were harassing the Japanese mainland at extreme range, while in American hands it could become a splendid forward air base. In the event D-Days were set for Luzon, 9 January 1945, Iwo Jima, 19 February and Okinawa, 1 April.

Meantime the Japanese had been working on a new defense line to keep the Allies well away from the Japanese home islands. This defense line included Iwo Jima, Okinawa, Taiwan, Shanghai and South Korea. In these areas Japanese ground forces were to hold out to the end without reinforcements. Suicide aircraft – called Kamikaze after the 'divine wind' which had thwarted the last attempted invasion of Japan in the thirteenth century – would be used against the advancing enemy. The final battle would be fought in Japan itself, and bloody attrition was expected to bring the Americans to terms.

On Iwo Jima Major General Tadamichi Kuribayashi commanded a garrison of some 22,000 Japanese army and naval troops. The island itself was honeycombed with concealed gun emplacements, concrete pillboxes and expertly interlaced minefields. An elaborate underground cave system protected Kuribayashi's men against the incessant bombardments which preceded the American assault. This began at 0900 hours on 19 February when men of the 4th and 5th US Marine Divisions landed without much opposition until they got clear of the beaches. Then the Japanese artillery opened up and the Marines suffered heavy casualties – 2420 men on the first day. However the attackers inched forward, under cover of naval gunfire which provided continuous and accurate support. Mount Suribachi, the dominant feature of the island, was stormed on 23 February and the photograph of the American flag being raised on its crest became one of the best-known pictures of the war. By 11 March the remnants of the defenders were pinned on the northern tip of the island and organized resistance ended on 16 March.

The Kamikaze corps was four months old when the Iwo Jima campaign opened and it had made its debut in the Philippines. There, in terms of men and materiel, the Kamikazes had exacted a terrible toll from the Americans – not so great as they believed at the time, but nonetheless formidable. Nothing like this had ever been known before and although the

Americans were not daunted they were shocked by such savage tactics. On 21 February a massive suicide attack was launched against the American invasion fleet off Iwo Jima. Early in the morning 32 Kamikazes took off from airfields near Tokyo and launched their attack. That night Tokyo radio announced that a US aircraft carrier and four transports had been sunk and another carrier and four other warships had been damaged. Subsequently the Americans confirmed that the carrier USS *Bismarck Sea* had been sunk and the carriers *Saratoga* and *Lunga Point*, together with a cargo ship and two landing ships, had been damaged.

The attacks were an indication of things to come. By the way Japanese resistance was mounting the Americans could look forward to nothing less than a suicidal blood bath on their way to Tokyo. Iwo Jima cost the lives of 6891 US Marines and 18,070 others were wounded. Japanese casualties were even heavier. Only 212 of the garrison surrendered and more than 21,000 dead were counted; many others were sealed in their underground shelters. It is hardly surprising therefore that the

Left: A Coast Guard-manned LST heads for the beach at Leyte in the Philippines, where an American force landed in October 1944.
Below: Iwo Jima was assaulted in February 1945. Men of the 5th Marine Division are having an especially difficult time in establishing themselves ashore.
Above: A Japanese position at the base of Mount Suribachi is bombarded.

occupation of Okinawa, the next step to Japan, was viewed with some trepidation. Okinawa is the central and largest island of a long chain commonly known as the Ryukyu Archipelago. It is only 340 miles from both the Japanese home island of Kyushu, and Taiwan; 900 miles from Leyte, and 1200 miles from Ulithi and Guam which, early in 1945, were the three nearest US bases. Pearl Harbor lies 4000 miles to the east. Strategically Okinawa dominated the East China Sea and the Chinese coast from Foochow to Korea. It sat astride Japan's sea lanes to the oil-rich East Indies. Furthermore, from Okinawa American B-29s would be able to range over the Yellow Sea and Straits of Shimonseki and return with fuel to spare.

Okinawa was a natural defensive stronghold. Sixty-seven miles long and from 3–20 miles wide, its terrain was cut up in a maze of ridges, cliffs, and limestone and coral caves. Divided into two by the narrow Ishikawa Isthmus, the larger, northeastern portion of the island is barren, mountainous and thickly wooded. Immediately south of the isthmus the terrain is undulating and lightly wooded and the southwestern end is rugged and hilly. In 1945 three-quarters of the island's population of 435,000 lived in the area south of the isthmus. The capital was located there and in this southern part of the island the Japanese had constructed three airfields – at Naha, Yontan and at Kadena close to the west coat. In addition there were two other airstrips, at Yonabaru and Machinato. Nakagusuku Wan (Buckner Bay) and Chimu, the two extensive bays on the eastern side of Okinawa, were considered suitable for development into an advanced naval base since both were protected from the sea by clusters of small islands and barrier reefs. Across the straits, some 11 miles west of Naha, lies a group of 10 small islands known as the Kerama Retto, and off the point of the Motobu Peninsula in the northern part of Okinawa, is the island of Ie-Shima on which there was another small airfield.

The people of Okinawa are descended from a mixture of Chinese, Malays and Ainus. At one time they were an independent kingdom whose ruler paid tribute to the emperor of China. In 1875, however, the Ryukyu islands were invaded by the Japanese who deposed the king, stopped the tribute to China and formally annexed the territory. The colonial-type regime which was then introduced did not endear the islanders to their Japanese masters, who treated them as inferior beings. In the event this eased the task of the US troops in dealing with the Okinawans when they discovered that the stories of American brutality told to them by the Japanese were untrue.

Compared with Japan the islands were underdeveloped and overpopulated. There were only three towns of any size – Naha, the capital; Shuri, the ancient capital; and Toguchi on the Motobu Peninsula.

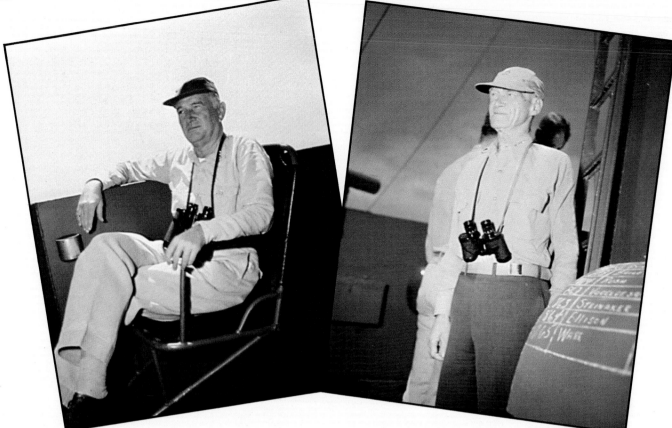

Above: Vice-Admiral Marc Mitscher commanded the aircraft-carrier task force which supported the Okinawa landings.
Above left: Rear Admiral Jesse Oldendorf on the bridge of the battleship USS *Tennessee.* He was an exponent of traditional surface-ship action.
Below left: Admirals C Nimitz (right) and R Spruance tour Kwajalein.

Most Okinawans lived in thatched huts, clustered in villages of a few hundred or so inhabitants. They were predominantly farmers, raising barley, sugar cane, cabbages and sweet potatoes – the latter providing the staple of their diet while pork was the principal luxury. (An ancient law still in force in 1945 required each family to keep four pigs.)

Such, in sum, is the nature of the island which was needed as a springboard to Japan, and the invasion of which would cost the United States more casualties than had been incurred in taking any other of the islands in the Pacific.

Preparations for Operation Iceberg, the invasion of the Ryukyus, started in October 1944 and from the very beginning it was clear that this would be the most daring and the most complex operation ever undertaken by American amphibious forces. Lieutenant General Buckner's Tenth US Army, consisting of the III Amphibious Corps (1st, 2nd and 6th Marine Divisions) and the XXIV Corps (7th, 27th, 77th and 96th Divisions with the 81st held in reserve in New Caledonia) would be put ashore on Okinawa on 1 April. Most of the troops concerned were seasoned veterans, having already taken part in similar operations elsewhere in the Pacific. As the objective was so far from the Allied airfields and was surrounded by Japanese airfields within a 350-mile radius, Buckner planned to make the initial landing on the west of the island on the Hagushi beaches,

Below: Lieutenant General Simon Bolivar Buckner (left) talks with amphibious-warfare expert Vice-Admiral R Kelly Turner.

in order to secure the Yontan and Kadena airfields quickly. As soon as they had been captured and the middle of the island cleared, the Marines would fan out east and north to occupy the island as far as the Motobu Peninsula and capture Ie-Shima with its airfield. Meantime the men of the XXIV Corps would turn south. Their task was to mop up the southern end of the island and occupy the cluster of islands on the east coast masking the entrance to the Chimu and Nakagusuku bays. About a week before the main assault, the Kerama Retto group of islands, which provided a large anchorage, was to be seized for use as an advanced fuelling and repair base and as a refuge for ships damaged during operations.

Under the overall command of Admiral Spruance the greatest invasion fleet ever to operate in the Pacific now began to assemble – 1440 warships and merchant ships of all kinds and sizes. This included Vice-Admiral Marc Mitscher's fast-carrier force of 11 fleet carriers, six light carriers, seven battleships, 15 cruisers and 64 destroyers, the British Pacific Fleet under the command of Vice-Admiral Sir Bernard Rawlings, and Vice-Admiral Turner's Joint Expeditionary Force.

The British Pacific Fleet comprised the battleships *King George V* and *Howe*, the fleet carriers *Indomitable, Victorious, Indefatigable* and *Illustrious,* five cruisers and 11 destroyers.

The Joint Expeditionary Force consisted of the Gun-Fire and Covering Force under command of Rear Admiral M L Deyo, Rear Admiral W H P Blandy's Amphibious Support Force, the Western Islands Attack Group carrying the 77th Division for the assault on the Kerama Retto, the Northern Attack Force carrying the 1st and 6th Marine Divisions, and the Southern Attack Force carrying the 7th and 96th Divisions. There were also two other small, self-contained forces – one to set up a seaplane base at the Kerama Retto when the islands had been captured, and the other carrying part of the 2nd Marine Division which was to make a diversionary landing on the east coast opposite Yonabaru airfield. Aboard this vast armada there were approximately 182,000 soldiers and Marines together with all their stores and supplies.

Before D-Day the Iceberg planners reckoned that a week of air bombardments would be necessary to 'soften up' the objective. Kamikaze air attacks were expected and so it was necessary to pare down Japanese air power as much as possible before the invasion of Okinawa started. The softening-up bombardments and air strikes against the Japanese airfields would be carried out mainly by planes from Mitscher's and Deyo's fast carriers. However, to assist them in the bombing program and in the formidable task of protecting the invasion armada against attack by Kamikazes the Joint Chiefs of Staff in

Washington authorized Nimitz to call on the Superfortress B-29 bombers of the Strategic Air Command based in the Marianas. (This, in fact, was not a popular arrangement so far as Generals 'Hap' Arnold and Curtis LeMay of the Strategic Air Command were concerned. They were reluctant to have the costly B-29s employed like this. In the event Nimitz got his way.)

The preliminary 'softening-up' program that was eventually agreed included attacks on airfields in Kyushu, shipping in Japan's Inland Sea and targets on Okinawa by the carrier-borne planes. The Superfortresses would thicken up the bombardments with attacks on Kyushu. They would also drop mines in the Shimonseki Strait through which most of Japan's remaining shipping then passed, as well as the approaches to Sagebo, Hiroshima and Kure. At the same time planes from the carriers of the British Pacific Fleet would bomb the airfields in the Sakishima Islands. The program would start on 18 March and continue through to the 26th when the Gunfire and Covering Force would join the lists to add their contribution to the forthcoming *Götter-dämmerung* with an intensified bombardment of Okinawa. Minesweepers, in the van of the Joint Expeditionary Force, were to begin to clear the approaches to Okinawa of mines on 22 March and the Western Attack Group was to assault the Kerama Retto on the 26th. Finally on D-Day the 1st and 6th Marine Divisions were to be landed just north of, and the 7th and 96th Divisions immediately south of, the Bisha River on the Hagushi beaches.

The Japanese knew the Americans would invade Okinawa, and indeed they guessed the correct date of D-Day. They were under no illusions – they had to defend successfully this malaria-ridden island or lose the war. Okinawa was so important that they were prepared to risk everything to hold it. Two divisions and two brigades of the Imperial Army under command of Lieutenant General Mitsura Ushijima were deployed mainly in the southern part of the island. There was also a naval force under Rear Admiral Minoru Ota, which included seven sea raiding companies manning *Shinyo* suicide boats (boats powered by a gasoline engine with an explosive charge in the bow), three companies were stationed in the Kerama Retto and the remainder in Okinawa. Originally there were seven battalions of *Shinyo*, but Ushijima reduced them to form three infantry battalions to supplement the army battalions. About 7000 airmen commanded by Captain Tanamachi were also available. These in fact were ground crews who had no aircraft to service. An Okinawa Home Guard some 20,000 strong provided labor units. All in all the total strength of the Japanese garrison – excluding civilians – was about 80,000 men.

That Kamikaze air attacks would be mounted against the invading force was a foregone conclusion. In addition to suicidal

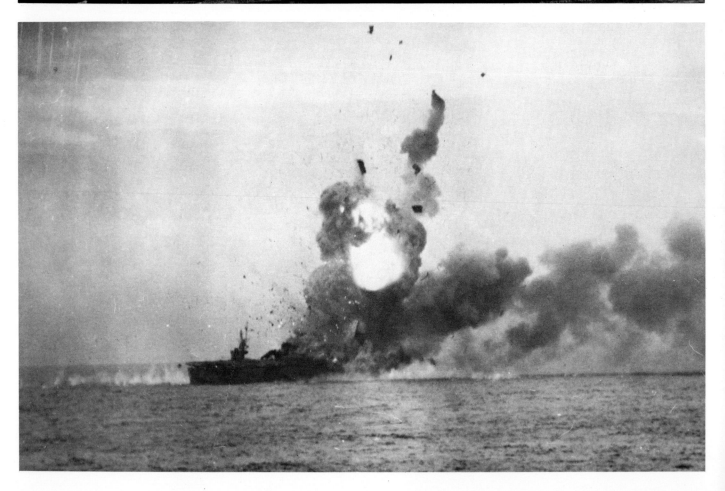

Above left: Curtiss SB2C Helldivers take off from the carrier USS *Enterprise* (CV-6) for a strike on Okinawa, October 1944.
Left: The escort carrier USS *St Lo* (CVE-63) under Kamikaze attack on 25 October 1944. The carrier sank later that day.

Above: The naval equivalent of the Kamikaze was the Kaiten human torpedo. This example was discovered on Ulithi Atoll in 1945.

attacks from the skies the Japanese also planned to strike under the sea with human torpedoes. In February 1944 they had developed a type of one-man midget submarine which its designers called the Kaiten (literally, 'Heaven shaker'). In essence it was simply an oversized torpedo which had an additional section between the warhead in the nose and the oxygen motor. This was the pilot's compartment, fitted with a periscope and a set of controls enabling a man to direct the torpedo run. The Kaiten had a range of 40 nautical miles and tests had shown that its 9000-pound high explosive warhead was capable of breaking the back of a heavy cruiser. The original design had included an escape hatch, giving the pilot a chance to get away once he had put his weapon on a sure course to the target. In mid-1944 the Naval General Staff decided to simplify the design to permit crash production of these weapons, and the Kaiten became another suicide weapon.

Like the Kamikaze airmen Kaiten pilots were all volunteers. Until they started their training none of them knew what they had volunteered for. They were merely told that they would operate a *Kyukoko heiki* – a new national salvation weapon – on missions from which they were not expected to return alive. Even when it was learned that their probable fate was an unseen death beneath the waves there were plenty of volunteers. Indeed, it appears that the first ones were grateful at being accepted. Selection was supposedly based on three qualifications: physical and moral strength, evidence of a strong sense of patriotism, and a minimum of family responsibilities. Married men were excluded and very few eldest or only sons were chosen. The accent was on young fit men who would have little tendency to look over their shoulders.

The Kaitens were carried to the operational area in big I Class fleet submarines, each of which was fitted to carry six. During the approach to the target the Kaiten pilots climbed into their tiny craft through a special hatch which was then sealed off. As the submarine closed on its victim, a telephone link between the submarine's conning tower and the Kaiten enabled the captain to keep the pilots informed of the relative position of the

target. At the optimum moment the Kaiten's engines were started and they were released at five-second intervals from the mother ship. Once in motion the pilot could observe the target through his own periscope, and make the necessary corrections to his course. At about 500 yards distance he would switch his craft to automatic control for the final dash at full speed, submerged to a depth of about 12 feet.

The first Kaiten attack was made in November 1944 at Ulithi Atoll. Three fleet submarines, each carrying four Kaiten, set out for the vicinity of Ulithi where large numbers of American ships were reported to be concentrating. En route the I-37 was spotted by the American destroyer *Nicholas* and sunk. The I-36 reached the position designated for launching its four Kaitens, just off the eastern entrance to the Ulithi lagoon, soon after midnight on 20 November. The pilots were ordered into their craft and everything seemed set for the attack when it was found that Numbers One and Two Kaiten were stuck in their racks, and Number Four reported his craft was leaking badly. Only Number Three, manned by Ensign Imanishi, could be dispatched and it was launched shortly before 0500 hours.

The third fleet submarine, the I-47, was more successful. All four of its Kaiten were launched successfully at about 0500 hours. Judging by the three explosions which were heard by the crew of the I-47, at least three of the Kaiten had scored hits on something. Nobody knew what damage they had done but one thing was certain; all five Kaiten pilots were dead. Both I-36 and I-47 got safely back to their home port of Kure and on 2 December a special conference was held on board the *Tsukushi Maru*, flagship of the Sixth Fleet, to consider the reports of the two submarine captains on the Kaiten attacks. Over 200 staff officers and specialists attended, and there was a lot of discussion before the results were summarized by a staff officer of the Sixth Fleet. Men on board I-47 had seen two fires, he said, and the crew of I-36 had heard explosions. Photographs of Ulithi taken by a reconnaissance plane from Truk on 23 November, three days after the Kaiten operation, were then produced. 'From these,' declared the speaker, 'we can estimate that Lieutenant Nishina sank an aircraft carrier, as did Lieutenant Fukuda and Ensign Imanishi. Ensigns Sato and Watanabe sank a battleship apiece!'

This was the conclusion the audience wanted to hear, and there was a great outburst of banzais. The Japanese High Command had ordered Kaiten to be produced in quantity, and news that the first strike had been an outstanding success was a great boost to the morale of the scores of young men in training. 'Die for the Emperor, but not in vain' was a good motto. Every embryo Kaiten pilot was positively

Left and below: Japanese midget submarines were used for local defense of strategically important bases in the closing years of the Pacific War.
Below left: The Yokosuka MXY-7 Ohka was a rocket-propelled suicide plane, which was carried to the vicinity of its target by a Mitsubishi G4M parent aircraft.

looking forward to his death-dealing mission after the news was circulated.

However the Japanese estimate of ships destroyed was a complete fabrication. The only ship sunk in the operation was the US tanker *Mississinewa.* Nevertheless the Kaiten represented yet another serious menace to the Allied armada currently assembling for the invasion of Okinawa.

Among other Japanese preparations to stop the seemingly irresistible American advance was the development of a new, simpler Kamikaze aircraft to supplement the dwindling stocks of fighter aircraft and reconnaissance planes that had been used up to this time. During the summer months of 1944 Ensign Ohta had come up with the idea of a piloted bomb which could be carried into action by a Type-O Betty bomber. The idea was taken up by the Japanese Naval Command and the first of the new piloted glide bombs started to roll off the production lines in October 1944. Named Ohkas, they were tiny single-seater aircraft which had rocket motors, and 2640 pounds of high explosive packed into

the nose. As airplanes their performance was strictly limited and the mother aircraft had to launch them within 10 miles of their target. From an altitude of 20,000 feet an Ohka had a range of about 15 miles and the pilots were taught to correct their glide path with short blasts of the rocket motors. The system was comparatively simple. En route to the combat zone the Ohka pilot travelled in the mother bomber. Approaching the target area he would climb through the bomb bay into his bomb, and when the pilot of the bomber had confirmed the target and aligned his plane the Ohka would be released. When this happened there was no return. It was a one-way ride for the Ohka pilot.

Like the more conventional Kamikaze pilots and the men who manned the Kaiten, the young men who flew the Ohkas were all volunteers. Most of them were youngsters who had only the minimal training necessary for their mission. However, as D-Day for Operation Iceberg approached they were joined by a few hard-bitten veterans from experienced units.

2. PRELIMINARY OPERATIONS

To isolate the battlefield the Americans planned to neutralize the Japanese airfields in southern Japan, and on 14 March Admiral Marc Mitscher's fleet – designated Task Force 58 – sailed from Ulithi and headed toward Kyushu. By dawn on the 18th Mitscher's carriers had reached their flying-off position some 90 miles southeast of Kyushu, and the planes took off to strafe the airfields on Kyushu. The Americans had expected to run into considerable opposition, but much to the surprise of the pilots there were very few Japanese planes either in the air or on the ground – for a very good reason. A Japanese reconnaissance plane had shadowed Task Force 58 from Ulithi, and Vice-Admiral Matome Ugaki, the Commander of the Fifth Air Fleet, had decided to launch a devastating air attack on the American carriers. In consequence when the US planes were flying toward Kyushu to drop their bombs on deserted airfields, all the available aircraft of the Fifth Air Fleet – including 50 torpedo bombers – were winging their way toward Mitscher's fleet. In the ensuing action the two fleet carriers *Enterprise* and *Yorktown* were hit by bombs. However neither ship suffered serious damage – although some men were killed or wounded. The Fifth Air Fleet not only lost many aircraft, it also became considerably disorganized as its surviving planes landed on airfields all over southern Japan.

The following day, 19 March, Mitscher's planes struck at Japanese shipping in the Inland Sea and at Kure and Kobe, and when they returned to their carriers they reported hits on 17 ships including such monsters as the battleship *Yamato* and the carrier *Amagi*. In fact, except for a cruiser, which was severely damaged, only minor damage had been inflicted. Meantime the Japanese had counterattacked and their efforts had been more successful. Two American carriers, the *Wasp* and the *Franklin* ('Big Ben' as her crew called her) had been hit by bombs and badly damaged. *Wasp* was attacked shortly after sunrise, soon after most of her aircraft had taken off on strikes. A solitary Japanese bomber was undetected until it was over the ship and dropped a bomb which smashed through to the lower deck where the cooks were preparing breakfast. A few minutes later a Kamikaze plane dived on the carrier and exploded as it crashed alongside. Casualties were heavy

– 101 killed and 269 wounded – and the *Wasp* eventually had to retire for repairs. 'Big Ben' was caught soon after 0700 hours as she was launching her second strike of the morning. Two bombs from a Japanese aircraft which also made an undetected approach were dropped to explode on the hangar and flight decks, creating a fire which quickly enveloped the entire ship in flames and a pall of heavy smoke. Everyone on the hangar deck was killed and in the blaze the bombs in the planes which were about to be launched blew up. The 'Tiny Tim' rockets, with which a dozen fighter bombers on the flight deck were armed, were also ignited and these produced a spectacular display. According to Commander Joe Taylor, the *Franklin*'s executive officer:

'Some screamed by to starboard, some to port, and some straight up the flight deck. The weird aspect of this weapon whooshing by so close is one of the most awful spectacles a human has ever been privileged to see. Some went straight up and some tumbled end over end. Each time one went off the fire-fighting crews forward would instinctively hit the deck.'

Before the fires were brought under control all the ammunition stored on the flight deck and in the hangar had exploded.

For a while it appeared as if the *Franklin* was doomed and the skipper, Captain Leslie H Gehres, ordered all but a skeleton crew to abandon ship. Many men dived overboard and were rescued by destroyers which had closed in on the stricken carrier. The wounded were taken off by the cruiser *Santa Fe* which ran alongside the blazing and exploding *Franklin* for that purpose.

In the event the men who remained aboard the crippled *Franklin* managed to bring the fires under control and by the morning of 21 March she was able to move under her own power. Her flight deck looked rather like a half-eaten Shredded Wheat biscuit, according to Captain Gehres, who reported 'Down by the tail but reins up.' To this Admiral Spruance signalled back that 'the ability, fortitude and sheer guts of skipper and crew in saving their ship were in the highest degree praiseworthy.'

The *Franklin* was the most heavily damaged Allied carrier in World War II to

Above: General Kazushige Ugaki was foreign minister in the first cabinet of Prince Konoye.
Right: USS *Intrepid* (CV-11) belches smoke after a Japanese air attack on 18 March 1945.
Above right and above far right: The carrier *Franklin* was severely damaged by Kamikazes on 19 March, but despite casualties of 724 killed and 265 wounded the ship remained afloat.

be saved; she was in far worse shape than the *Lexington* had been at the Coral Sea or the *Yorktown* at Midway. But she managed under her own power – with only one stop at Pearl Harbor – to make the 12,000-mile voyage to New York. She was lucky in the initial stages of her withdrawal. Following the Inland Sea strikes on 19 March the whole of Mitscher's Task Force 58 began slowly to retire, sending fighter sweeps over Kyushu to deter any Japanese aircraft.

The morning of 20 March was quiet, but the situation was brewing up. During the afternoon Kamikaze planes crashed down on the destroyer *Halsey Powell*. Fortunately the Kamikaze's bomb went right through the *Halsey Powell*'s hull without exploding, but 12 men were killed and the ship's steering gear put out of action.

Soon after this between 15-20 Japanese aircraft swooped down on Mitscher's fleet and one plane bombed and strafed the carrier *Enterprise*. The bombs missed and little damage was done. The climax was yet to come.

Task Force 58 was shadowed during the night and early on the morning of 21 March. Vice-Admiral Ugaki at Kyushu was handed a report from the pilot of one of the reconnaissance planes which had been following the US fleet. Three US carriers appeared to be wallowing in the water about 320 miles off Japan, the pilot reported. All three appeared to have suffered damage and, surprisingly, no fighter cover was being maintained; indeed they appeared to be completely unprotected.

Ugaki decided that this was the ideal opportunity to try out the Ohka. Eighteen bombers began to load Ohka weapons, and every available fighter in the whole of southern Japan was ordered up to escort the bombers. Carrying the heavy Ohkas the ponderous bombers would be slower than ever, and a powerful escort was necessary to make sure they got through to where the carriers had been sighted. Only 55 Zeros could be mustered, and because this was considered too few the operation was very nearly called off. According to the official report it was the enthusiastic determination and keenness of the Ohka pilots which resulted in the decision to take the risk and let the operation proceed.

Commanding the bombers was a certain Lieutenant Commander Goro Nonaka, one of the few veterans who remained. He was said to be a hard man, 'who placed great emphasis on the traditional Samurai spirit.' Nevertheless his unit was a happy one, and Nonaka was respected as an able leader.

Nonaka's senior was the 45-year-old Captain Okamura, who had grown gray in the service of the Imperial Navy's fleet air arm. It was he who had raised and organized the first Ohka unit, and he was determined to vindicate his work by taking part in the very first Ohka mission. When the aircraft were warming up Okamura announced that he was going to lead the attack. Nonaka was furious. He too was anxious to be the first Ohka martyr, and apparently there was a somewhat unseemly argument on the airstrip before Okamura gave way.

Nonaka had obviously prepared his last speech and before climbing into the cockpit of his bomber he announced enigmatically, 'This is Minatogawa.' (The reference was to the shrine of that name at Kobe, which was erected to immortalize the fourteenth-century patriot Masashige Kusunoki who said before his death 'Shichisei hokoku!' – Would that I had seven lives to give for my country!)

The 18 bombers took off at 1135 hours with Nonaka leading. All the pilots were wearing the customary *hachimaki* and as this was one of the biggest and most important operations for some time, the

Below: Firefighters at work on the flight deck of USS *Enterprise* spray foam around the Hellcats of Air Group 90.
Right: A formation of Grumman TBM Avengers approaches the coast of Okinawa during the preinvasion bombardment phase.
Bottom: A destroyer escort drops depth charges near a Japanese submarine, which penetrated Ulithi Harbor in November 1944.

So ended the first of the Ohka sorties. The American airmen claimed to have destroyed 528 aircraft in the air and on the ground in these operations and the Japanese admitted later that 'losses had been staggering': 161 planes was their figure. Indeed they were so staggering that the Japanese Air Force was not able to participate effectively in the defense of Okinawa until 6 April. Admiral Ugaki, however, claimed that his 'eagles' had sunk five carriers, two battleships and three cruisers, and that the Americans would have to postpone their attack on Okinawa.

Although they must have known better, the Japanese appear to have accepted Ugaki's claim. On 23 March planes from Admiral Mitscher's carriers started their prelanding bombing program of targets on Okinawa and Admiral Blandy's ships appeared in the Kerama Retto. The Japanese High Command assumed that the bombing was a Parthian shot from crippled carriers returning to Ulithi and that Blandy's force was some sort of diversion. Within two days they knew better and an all-out air attack on Blandy's ships was ordered. By that time it was too late to interfere with the landings and the concentrated air attack did not materialize until 6 April.

Meantime the battlefield-isolation program was continuing as planned. On 27 and 31 March the B-29s of the US Army Air Force hammered the airfields in Kyushu, Taiwan and Honshu; they also dropped mines in the Shimonoseki Strait, effectively closing the main Japanese supply line for over a week. Finally the part played by the British Pacific Fleet deserves a brief mention. On 26 and 27 March and again from 30 March–2 April planes from the four British carriers attacked airfields in the Sakishima Islands and coastal shipping. During the time the British fleet was in action it was attacked by Kamikaze aircraft, and the carrier *Indefatigable* and the destroyer *Ulster* were both hit. The steel decks of the carrier prevented serious damage, but the destroyer had to be towed back to Ulithi for repairs. Operation Iceberg was now under way and during and after the landings the British carriers provided a flying buffer between the American amphibious forces and the Japanese airfields on Sakishima.

Concentrating Vice-Admiral Kelly Turner's invasion fleet during the latter half of March was no mean feat of organization. No single assembly area was big enough for this vast armada. Leyte Gulf was ample for the Northern Attack Force which was to land the Marines on the northern Hagushi beaches, but even the big lagoon at Ulithi was insufficient to hold the Southern Attack Force which was to land the troops on the southern Hagushi shoreline. The fact that other ships supporting the operation could only use the facilities at Ulithi served to complicate matters still further. So components of the invasion fleet had to move according to a

edge of the runway was lined with spectators from the base. Admiral Ugaki himself was there to see the Kamikazes off, with tears in his eyes, it was said. Maybe his tears were for the brave men who would not return; possibly his thoughts were centered on the wretched depths to which his country had sunk. The takeoff was a depressing spectacle. Of the 55 Zeros assembled for escort duty, eight could not even get off the ground to follow the lumbering bombers, and 17 others were forced to turn back along the way because of engine trouble. No sooner were the planes airborne than a reconnaissance plane reported that the American carriers, surrounded by many more warships than was originally believed, had separated and the various groups were heading southwest.

With news like this the chance of the Kamikazes' success was considerably reduced, and there was some argument on whether the operation should be called off before the planes got any further. While Ugaki hesitated, 50 Grumman fighters settled the issue. The escorting Zeros tried in vain to drive off the interceptors, who concentrated their efforts on the Ohka-laden bombers. In consequence the bombers, powerless to fight back effectively, had to jettison their Ohkas to lighten their load and increase their maneuverability. Even so, 14 of them were shot down in quick succession, and nothing more was seen or heard of the others after they dived into a cloud bank hotly pursued by Grummans.

Top: From November 1944 the Japanese homeland came under attack from Boeing B-29 Superfortresses based in the Marianas. A B-29 of the 40th Bomb Group, 20th Air Force, is shown.
Above: The A6M5 variant of the Zero fighter was introduced into service in 1943 and fought until the end of the war.
Far right: The Curtiss SB2C Helldiver was never a popular aircraft with its crews, but the dive bomber played an important role in the naval air war in the Pacific.

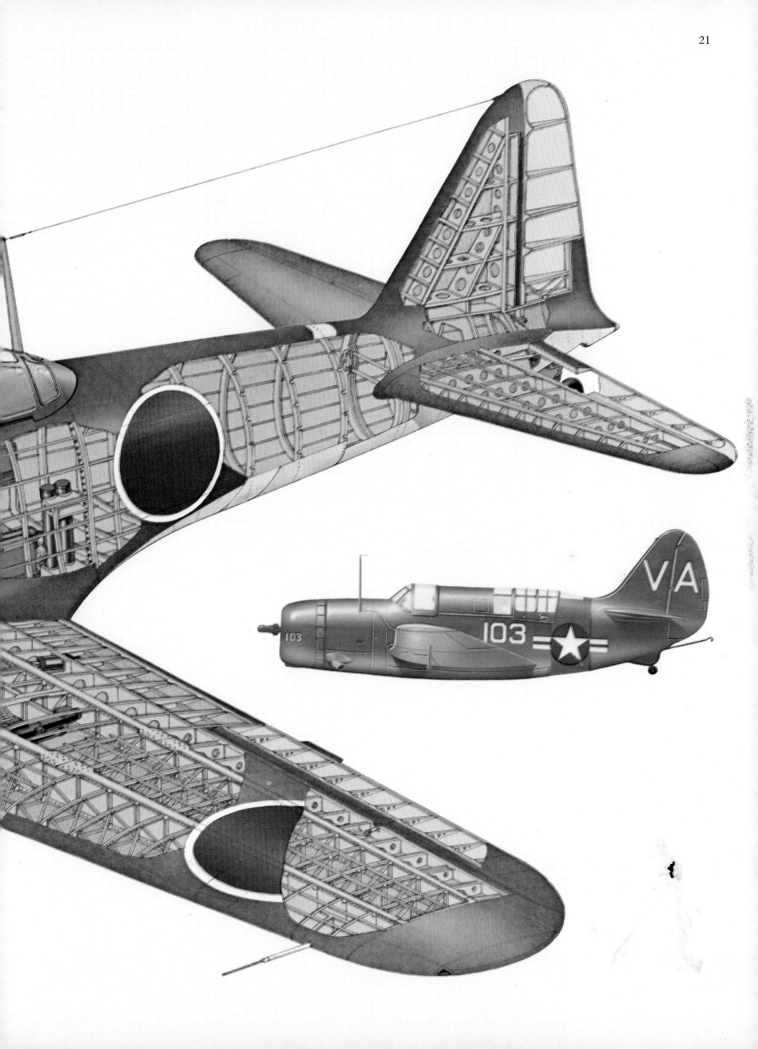

strict schedule. Some of the ships which had been supporting the operation on Iwo Jima were badly in need of overhaul, and their crews needed rest and time to recuperate. There was no time; ships were refuelled and replenished and then they had to leave their berths for other vessels to take their place. Ulithi lagoon at this time was, in US Navy parlance, a 'hot bunk.'

Every effort was made to give the men who passed through Ulithi a memorable break and the atmosphere at the crowded officers club on the atoll on 20 March has been compared to the famous ball at Brussels on the eve of Waterloo. To boogie-woogie music played by a band of colored Seabees, officers of the US Navy and a few of their British counterparts danced with nurses from the three hospital ships, *Solace*, *Relief* and *Comfort*, lying in the lagoon. For some of them it would be their last dance, except for a dance of death with the Kamikaze Samurai. Next morning Rear Admiral 'Spike' Blandy's fire-support fleet, preceded by the minesweeping flotilla and its escort ships sailed for the Ryukyus, and were followed by the two assault forces – one of which had previously assembled in Leyte Gulf.

From Ulithi it was a run of only four days and the leading minesweepers sighted the peak of Kuba Shima in the Kerama Retto shortly after dawn on 24 March. From then on their task began in earnest, although some mines had already been encountered before they reached this point. Working in groups of four or five – each group under the protection of a destroyer – the minesweepers started methodically to sweep the ocean off Okinawa. The importance of their work may be gauged from the slogan coined by the minesweepers themselves: 'No Sweep, No Invasion.' If any warning were needed of the awful hazards associated with mines, what happened to the destroyer *Halligan* provided it. Venturing into unswept waters close to the shore, the *Halligan* hit a mine which blew up the ship's forward magazines. Altogether 153 men were killed and another 39 wounded out of a total complement of 325.

Nor were mines the only hazards the vessels of the minesweeping flotilla had to contend with. They were under constant air attack, day and night, and as the operation progressed more and more of them were sunk or damaged by Kamikazes. A number of submarine 'contacts' were also detected. Most of these were written off as false alarms, but it is possible that an attempt was made to pick off the odd destroyer with a Kaiten. The Japanese fleet submarine *I-44* captained by Commander Genbei Kawaguchi was sent out with a full complement of Kaiten to inflict as much

damage as possible. He failed. According to the report Kawaguchi submitted on his return to the submarine's base at Otsujima the American antisubmarine patrols were operating everywhere and every time he tried to surface the *I-44* was detected. After US planes and ships had compelled him to remain submerged for 48 hours Kawaguchi called off the operation. For this he was relieved of his command; the Imperial Navy had little patience with officers who failed. Kawaguchi had thought it better to live and fight another day; his superiors did not agree with him.

While the minesweepers were still sweeping channels toward the main objective, the next phase of Operation Iceberg was initiated. This was the occupation of the group of mountainous islands known as the Kerama Retto which lies 15 miles west of southern Okinawa. The islands were thinly populated and the Japanese garrison was estimated to be about a thousand strong. (In the event this proved to be an exaggeration.)

An approach to the islands had been cleared by the minesweepers by 25 March when a couple of cruisers, the *San Francisco* and *Minneapolis*, and five destroyers moved in to bombard the beaches and Japanese defense works on the central island. Under cover of this bombardment frogmen went in to reconnoiter the approaches to the beaches which men of the US 77th Division would assault the following day. Landing craft lifted the frogmen to points about 500 yards from the shore where they took to the water from where they swam in toward the beach taking soundings at regular intervals.

Early next morning the *San Francisco* and *Minneapolis* and their accompanying destroyers resumed the bombardment of the beaches and defenses, and the fire from their guns was augmented by the 12-inch guns of the 33-year-old battleship *Arkansas*. Then shortly after first light planes from the escort carriers screamed in to bomb and strafe the landing zones. Meanwhile the amphibious and landing craft carrying the troops were moving in and the landings were effected exactly as planned, and without the loss of a single man. The Japanese had been taken completely by surprise; they had never thought that the Americans would be interested in the Kerama Retto. The Japanese soldiers there – and there were only a few hundred of them – herded the local population into caves and tunnels and prepared to die fighting. They did attempt two counterattacks during the first day, but the American beachheads were firmly established and the Japanese suffered heavy casualties and gained nothing. After that there was no organized resistance and such as there was was sporadic. On one of the smaller islands a dozen local women and a few children were found dead in a cave. They had been strangled by their own menfolk who had been told that a fate worse than death awaited them at the hands of the brutal

and licentious American soldiers. The murderers were captured and when they found out what the Americans were really like they begged their guards to permit them to 'take it out' on the Japanese prisoners.

All the islands of the Kerama group had been occupied by the afternoon of 26 March, and work began on the establishment of a seaplane base. Nets covering the entrances to the roadstead were quickly laid also, to protect the vessels at anchor there from Kaiten attacks. Priority was given to the installation of antiaircraft and radar defenses, it appeared they were going to hit back with their Kamikazes. Sure enough the first attack came in the early evening of 26 March when nine Kamikaze aircraft attempted to crash dive on to ships of the invasion force. Next morning two other Kamikaze pilots flying obsolescent aircraft arrived on the scene and the destroyer *Kimberley* was slightly damaged but not disabled.

There was only one attempt to use a 'suicide boat' and one of the unexpected and welcome bonuses for the Americans was the capture of about 250 of these boats which had been camouflaged and concealed in caves on the Kerama Retto. The one attack that was made took place on the night of 28 March against the tender *Terebinth*. The crew saw the suicide boat racing toward them and prepared for the worst. However, it seemed that the Japanese pilot had no stomach for glory. After merely dropping one of the two 250-pound depth charges which these boats carried he veered away and raced off into the darkness – presumably to rejoin his comrades on Okinawa.

Back in Japan however, the staff of the Japanese Sixth Fleet were planning a more determined attack. The Japanese naval command still believed that the Kaiten could inflict enormous damage if employed properly. Following Kawaguchi's abortive mission, however, the commander and staff of the Sixth Fleet – responsible for the coordination and organization of Kaiten operations – had decided that a mass attack was called for. Only four of the fleet submarines capable of carrying Kaiten now remained. But it was proposed to fit them out to take as many as possible and they would all sail together to attack the American armada off Okinawa. A kind of underwater Banzai charge was envisaged, and the Japanese planners were convinced that some of the Kaiten must get through to their targets.

The operation was scheduled for the end of March, and the so-called Tatara Group (Tatara beach in northern Kyushu is where the Mongol armada was wrecked by the Kamikaze typhoon) of Kaiten pilots was embarked on the *I-44*, *I-47*, *I-56* and *I-58*. The *I-47* was designated the flagship for the Tatara operation. Three of the submarines carried four Kaiten, and the *I-56* had been refitted to take six.

The Kaiten pilots were given a party on the night of 26 March. A lot of sake was drunk, and Admiral Nagai, the commander of the Sixth Fleet, wished the Kaiten men 'every success.' 'I hope each of you will strike our enemy,' he said. 'At that moment your souls will fly to Yasukuni, there to watch forever over God's country, Japan. Please be assured that the rest of us in Sixth Fleet will do everything possible to comfort those you leave behind. . . .' Other senior officers made similar speeches exhorting the 'Samurai of the Sea' to 'do a good job.' Next morning, when they embarked, there were a few thick heads in the group.

In the event, like the previous operation, the Tatara affair was a complete and utter failure. Even as the submarine pack approached the target area the Americans were storming ashore at Okinawa, and no less than 150 destroyers were screening the vast invasion fleet. Through this formidable barrier of antisubmarine patrols the Japanese submarines had little hope of penetrating. *I-44* and *I-57* were sunk in the attempt. *I-47* managed to escape and limp back to Japan, and *I-58* was chased off and compelled to withdraw. There were now not enough submarines to take out all the men who were being trained to handle Kaiten, and by April most of them were

Below right: Inshore fire support was provided by suitably modified LCIs, such as this rocket-armed craft of the amphibious support force.
Below: A cruiser of the naval bombardment force in action. The landings on Okinawa were preceded by five days of naval and air bombardment.

scheduled to be employed in what was fancifully called 'base Kaiten attack.' A plan was drawn up for Kaiten to be deployed along Japan's coast, at points where an amphibious assault could most likely be expected. The Kaiten pilots were expected to hide their weapons and wait. When the Americans were just offshore, they would receive a signal from Imperial Headquarters. Then, the base Kaitens would roar out to sea and sink as many troopships as possible. Japanese naval strategy had not changed – give the Americans a blood bath and smash them in one single decisive action. This was the strategy that had been used at Midway, the Marianas and the Philippines. Soon it would be used again at Okinawa. It had not yet worked to Japan's advantage but as the Americans closed in, and the suicidal patriotic fervor increased, hopes that it might do so remained high.

The final 'softening-up' barrage of Okinawa began on 26 March and continued through until the 31st. The 16-inch guns of three *Maryland* Class battleships, 14-inch guns of two *New Mexico* Class and the old *New York*, *Texas* and *Tennessee*, augmented by the 12-inch armament of the *Arkansas* all combined fearsome firepower. To this was added the guns of seven heavy cruisers,

three light cruisers and 24 destroyers and over 50 rocket and mortar ships. Plenty of fire support for the prelanding bombardment was thus available. The problem was to select profitable targets. Clearly it was not possible to destroy every Japanese installation on such a big island before the troops landed even if it was feasible to pinpoint them. A study of the air photographs taken in March revealed that the Japanese appeared to have very few defensive works immediately behind the beaches on which the Americans would land. Consequently it was decided that the ships' gunfire would best be directed by aerial spotters flying over the island.

The Fire Support Force, as this prelanding bombardment fleet was called, closed on Okinawa during the late evening of 26 March. It was under the command of Rear Admiral Morton L Deyo, a 57-year-old dynamic character, and to date it was the biggest gunfire and covering force that had ever been concentrated for an operation in the Pacific. Steaming at 10 knots in four close columns it moved through the 10-mile wide channel between Tonaki and the Kerama Retto which the minesweepers had cleared and marked with radar reflecting buoys. It was a pleasantly cool night and only the distant

roll of artillery fire somewhere in the Kerama Retto indicated the presence of the Japanese. Those who had taken part in some of the earlier island-hopping expeditions knew that the enemy rarely showed his hand at the start of an operation.

At dawn the four columns of ships deployed for their bombardment tasks, with the battleships and cruisers remaining well offshore in waters that had been swept clean by the minesweepers. When they opened fire the only response evoked from the island's defenders was a burst of anti-aircraft fire which damaged one of the spotter planes. However, it became clear that Japanese submarines were somewhere around lying in wait when lookouts on board one of the cruisers reported seeing the wake of a torpedo; soon after the two other cruisers reported near misses by torpedoes.

Both submarines and Kamikaze attacks had been expected, and to cope with the latter it had been arranged that the escort carriers would provide an umbrella of fighter aircraft – first over the Fire Support Force and subsequently over the ships carrying the troops who were to land on the beaches. (This fighter cover was in addition to the bombing and strafing missions carried out by other carrier-based

aircraft.) This arrangement was to continue until one or other of the Japanese airfields was captured and put into commission so enabling land-based planes to take over. It worked well, not quite so well at the very beginning perhaps, but on and after 6 April when the Kamikazes attacked in alarming strength the carrier-based fighters accounted for more Japanese planes than did the ships' antiaircraft fire. Without them the invasion fleet would undoubtedly have suffered appalling casualties.

Unfortunately the air umbrella was not in position at dawn on the morning of 27 March when seven Kamikazes attacked. Diving through the curtain of antiaircraft fire one crashed onto the main deck of the battleship *Nevada*, knocking out two 14-inch guns, killing 11 men and wounding 49. A second Kamikaze narrowly missed the *Tennessee*, a third splashed down near the cruiser *Biloxi*, just before a fourth crashed into the side of the *Biloxi*. Fortunately for the crew the Kamikaze's bomb failed to explode and there were no casualties – other than the Japanese pilot. The destroyer *O'Brien*, hit by the fifth Kamikaze, was not so lucky; she lost 28 men killed, 22 missing and 76 wounded and had to return to the United States for repairs. The sixth Kamikaze crashed onto the deck of the minesweeper *Dorsey* but she got off with minor damage and only a few casualties. What happened to the seventh Kamikaze is not recorded, but it is presumed that the pilot joined his ancestors at Yasukuni.

During the six days of softening-up bombardment there was little variation in the routine followed by the Fire Support Force. Soon after sunrise, which was about 0630 hours, the ships would take up their positions and steam slowly down parallel to the shore, firing at targets behind the landing beaches – the targets being observed by the spotter aircraft who radioed back corrections to the gunlayers. Sunset was about 1845 hours, and about two hours before this the battleships and cruisers would retire seaward zigzagging to a rendezvous some 10-15 miles off Okinawa. There they would form a kind of seaborne laager for antiaircraft protection. The following morning they would return and resume the bombardment.

Between midnight on 28 March and dawn the following morning Japanese aircraft based on the Okinawa airfields tried to knock out the minesweepers working close to the coast. Only one of the US craft was damaged but the raiders caused a few casualties – at a cost to themselves of 10 aircraft. In the morning the crew of one of the minesweepers saw a man on the beach waving frantically. He appeared to be a European so the word was passed back and a seaplane was sent to pick him up. The seaplane alighted on the water just beyond the reef which precluded boats getting really close in, taxied in toward the beach and the rescue was successfully accom-

Above: A Vought F4U-ID Corsair of VF-10 'The Grim Reapers' from USS *Intrepid* patrols off Okinawa on 10 April 1945.

Right: A US Marine watches landing craft assemble for the assault on Okinawa. The Kerama Retto islands provided a jumping-off point for the main landings.

plished. The man concerned was a Lieutenant F M Fox of the *Yorktown* who had crashed while on a mission and had spent three days hiding near Kadena airfield.

That same day (29 March) a reconnaissance was made of the Hagushi beaches where the assault troops proposed to land and the beaches where they would pretend to land. The same technique was used as at Kerama Retto. Frogmen were taken to the reef in landing craft and from there they swam forward, taking soundings as they went. Except for some desultory mortar fire and sniping the Japanese did not respond. The fact that they did not do so made the Americans uneasy; this was not the way the enemy had reacted elsewhere. However, the frogmen returned and the results of the reconnaissance were assessed. The amphibious vehicles with which the

vanguard of the invaders would charge onto the beaches should be able to negotiate the reef without difficulty. In some places there would be enough water over the reef at high tide to float landing craft. The only obstacles the frogmen had encountered were about 3000 antiboat stakes which had been driven into the coral in an attempt to make it more of an obstacle. Next day, 30 March (Good Friday) the frogmen went back and under cover of a bombardment put down on the beaches by the destroyers and cruisers, they set about destroying these stakes. Working their way systematically along the reef the frogmen placed explosive charges timed to explode when they had returned to their landing craft. Once again the operations of the frogmen evoked no response from the Japanese.

Okinawa at this time appeared to be

completely deserted. The fields had been neatly cultivated but not a single human being or animal was to be seen either from the ships or from the air. Nobody moved on the roads and the villages appeared to be empty. If there were any military installations on the island it looked as if they had been most effectively camouflaged. American Intelligence said that there were at least 60,000 Japanese troops on Okinawa, but there was no indication of where they were. In consequence the invaders had the uncomfortable feeling that the Japanese were preparing a very nasty surprise.

Judging by Air reconnaissance reports, Ie Shima, the tiny island with the airfield lying north of Okinawa, was also deserted, and a Japanese officer rescued from a motor torpedo boat sunk in the area supported the delusion by insisting that it had been evacuated. Air photographs indicated that the airfield had taken a severe pounding and could not be used. As at Okinawa there was nobody to be seen and American planes flying low over Ie Shima were not fired upon. Two weeks later the US 77th Division had to kill about 3000 Japanese to secure the island.

Locating military installations on Okinawa seemed to be like seeking the proverbial needle in the haystack. However on 30 March air photographs of Unten-Ko – the reef-ringed harbor on Okinawa's Motobu Peninsula – disclosed the existence of a midget-submarine base. An immediate attack by planes from the escort carriers was ordered and the submarine pens were duly destroyed together with the midget submarines and motor torpedo boats housed in them. For the Americans the success was marred only by the fact that two aircraft failed to return from the raid. The attack wiped out all the midget submarines in the area.

All the evidence suggested that the Japanese had pulled back from the shoreline. Nevertheless the Americans expected the landing to be opposed. The Hagushi beaches were bisected by the Bishi River which flowed into the sea between two high and steep limestone banks, the faces of which were honeycombed with caves and tunnels. Machine guns emplaced in these caves could rake the landing beaches from end to end and were inaccessible to naval gunfire or air attack. Another limestone outcrop also honeycombed with caves commanded the southern beaches, and a concrete pillbox had been constructed to cover the beaches north of the river. Behind each of the beaches there was a thick six–10 feet high wall of masonry and concrete on which the naval gunfire had made little impression. One or two other concrete emplacements which were visible from the air had been badly battered, but the Americans felt that they had only touched the tip of the iceberg so far as military installations were concerned, and it looked as if the landings on the Hagushi were going to be a bloody business.

OCCUPIED BY US TENTH ARMY
19 APRIL

MAIN JAPANESE DEFENCE LINE
('SHURI LINE')

JAPANESE COUNTERATTACKS 4/5 MAY

AIRFIELDS

MILES 20

KILOMETRES 30

Hedo Pt
HEDO
13 Apr

6 Marine
Div

20 April
Taken by 6 Marine Div

AHA
19 Apr

IE SHIMA
BISE
12 Apr

TAKO

YAGACHI

TAIRA
11 Apr

16/21 April
77 Inf Div

Motobu Pen

▲*Yae
Take*

8 Apr

NAGO

EAST CHINA SEA

ATSUTA

8 Apr

'ICEBERG'
1 April 1945
US Tenth Army
(Buckner)

ONNA
4 Apr

KUSHI

27 Inf Div (Griner)
as floating reserve

*Ishikawa
Isthmus*

KIN

Okinawa

Chimu Bay

III Amph
Corps
(Geiger)

6 Marine Div

1 Marine Div

Yontan

HAGUSHI

*Katchin
Pen*

TAKABANARE

XXIV
Corps
(Hodge)

7 Inf Div

96 Inf Div

Kadena

HEANNA

PACIFIC OCEAN

Hagushi Bay
19 Apr

KUBA
4 Apr

10/11 April
Bn of 27 Div

TSUGEN
SHIMA

KEISE SHIMA

*Nakagusuku
Bay*

4 June
6 Marine Div

NAHA

SHURI

YONABARU

*Oruku
Pen*

**Jap Thirty-second
Army** (Ushijima)

ITOMAN

MINATOGA

MABUNI

21 May
Japanese withdraw
from 'Shuri Line'

KIYAMU

1/2 April
Demonstrations
by 2 Marine Div

21 June
End of Japanese resistance

Below left: Antiaircraft gunners aboard the battleship *West Virginia* keep watch by their 40mm weapons off Okinawa.
Bottom: Landing craft head for the Okinawa beaches on L-day, the first day of the assault.
Below: Lookouts scan the skies for incoming Kamikaze aircraft from their post aboard an American battleship.

3. OPERATION ICEBERG

At 0830 hours on the morning of Easter Sunday, 1 April 1945 the Americans stormed ashore on the Hagushi beaches. The weather had been slightly overcast and cool at 0630 hours when the assault troops prepared for H-Hour, and peered at the island which they had been told was likely to prove a tougher nut to crack than Iwo Jima. The cool weather was in fact a pleasant change for Marines and GIs who were accustomed to fighting in the steaming heat of the Philippines. As they climbed into their landing craft and amphibious vehicles however, the sun rose over the low-lying cloud. It was a beautiful morning and a perfect day for an amphibious operation: a calm sea and just enough wind to blow away the smoke of battle.

Four divisions were committed to the initial assault – two Marine (the 1st, veterans of Guadalcanal and Peleliu and the 6th, going into battle for the first time), and two infantry divisions (the 7th, veterans of Attu, Kwajalein and Leyte and the 96th, veterans of Leyte). The two Marine divisions each landed on five selected Hagushi beaches north of the Bishi River which served as an easily recognizable boundary between the Marine and Army divisions; the two infantry divisions landed on a total of 11 specified beaches south of the river.

Like previous Pacific-island invasions the landings had to be made over the fringing coral reef that extended seaward to a distance of eight to 12 hundred yards. There was one gap in the reef where the Bishi River flowed into the sea, but the Japanese were expected to have this so well covered with fire that it would be unusable until the suspected strongpoints in the bluff overlooking the gap had been cleared. The frogmen's reconnaissance had also shown that it would be possible to float small boats over the shelf-like reef at or near high water around 0900 hours. In the event the Americans went over the reef in amphibious vehicles and so well had the technique been developed as a result of previous operations that 700 odd amtracs landed some 8000 men in the first 20 minutes.

The landings followed the pattern which had been worked out for Saipan. Experience there and elsewhere had proved that ferrying troops from ship to shore in several hundred landing craft required a well-trained traffic-control group to supervise the operation. Officers and men of this group were naval personnel and they were equipped with motor boats. The selected beaches were all designated by colors and numbered – Green 1 and Green 2 for example. The 6th Marines were allotted two 'green' and three 'red' beaches, the 1st Marines two 'blue' and three 'yellow,' the 7th Infantry Division two 'purple' and two 'orange' and the 96th Division three 'white' and four 'brown' beaches. Control boats flying a flag corresponding to the beaches they controlled were deployed and anchored in front of the beaches an hour or so before the landings to indicate the direction in which the waves of landing craft should steer. To make absolutely certain that the first waves got to their correct beaches they were marshalled and led by fast motor boats flying appropriately colored pennants. Every landing craft of the initial waves also had the color of the beach for which it was destined painted on its topsides. The first troops ashore also set up colored beach markers, brightly painted canvas screens about 10 feet high.

While the landing craft and amphibious vehicles were moving in toward the beaches the ships of the naval support force bombarded the beach area along a 10-mile front lifting their fire only when the first wave of amtracs were some 75 yards from the shore. Meantime carrier-based strike aircraft continued the bombardment, raining bombs on targets which had been selected because they looked as if they might constitute Japanese strongpoints. The air was filled with noise – the sound of exploding bombs and drone of the aircraft motors being punctuated by repeated crashes as the battleships fired broadsides from their main armament. On board the *Tennessee* Admiral Deyo sniffed the yellow cordite fumes appreciatively and commented, 'That has a good offensive smell!'

The amphibians of the first wave hit the beaches at approximately 0830 hours, and waddled up toward the seawall. Behind them the second wave had already touched the shore; behind the second wave the third wave was crossing the reef and behind the third wave, the fourth, fifth, sixth and other waves were plowing in toward the reef. As far as the eye could see waves of landing craft were moving in toward Okinawa with majestic, precise deliberation.

Up to this point Japanese interest in the landing operations had been confined to a single Kamikaze attack on the naval armada.

31

Below: At 0832 hours the first assault wave hit the beaches.
Left: US Marines take cover after crossing the beaches.
Right: Marines move away from the beaches. By 1030 hours on L-day 50,000 men were ashore.

This was made at first light and the plane was shot down. There was nothing to indicate the presence of Japanese soldiers on the island until the landings were well under way. Then the first signs that the Japanese were there somewhere came when mortar bombs raised plumes of white water just off the beaches. Some of these bombs fell close to landing craft but none was hit and the warships went quickly into action. The fire was coming from mortars on the bluffs of the Bisha River, and a few ferocious salvos of naval gunfire quickly silenced them forever.

Apart from this minor bombardment the landings were completely unopposed. By 0900 hours the early morning mist had been completely dispersed and the sun was shining down on an incredible scene. Off shore the transports were continuing to discharge more men and vehicles to join the swarms of men and amphibians already on the beaches. Behind the beaches men and tanks were moving up the slopes toward the tableland of the interior; above them spotter planes circled, radioing back the troops' progress to headquarters.

By about 1030 hours some 50,000 men had landed on the island and the first waves of Marines had overrun both Yontan and Kadena airfields. They did not meet any opposition and had not suffered any casualties. Everybody was astounded and the questions on everybody's lips were: 'Where are the 60,000 or so Japanese that are supposed to be defending the island? And what about the elaborate defenses they were supposed to have constructed? Are we walking into some sort of trap – into a killing ground?' Throughout the afternoon

33

Left: Fleet Admiral Nimitz (left foreground) and Admiral Spruance tour the Okinawa beachhead.
Below left: LST-829 heads for the beaches with a floating causeway lashed alongside.

Below and bottom: As US troops moved inland on Okinawa they discovered that the Japanese garrison had withdrawn to the interior, leaving the old and sick and women and children to the invaders.

while the troops set about securing the hills dominating the two airfields, the total lack of opposition continued to puzzle the invaders. Behind the southern beaches there were a few bursts of mortar fire and some light artillery shells fell in the area through which the GIs of the 7th Division were advancing. On the northern beaches there was nothing, and intensive air reconnaissance failed to pick up any Japanese troop concentrations. In the late afternoon there was some sniping around Yontan airfield and three Japanese tanks were discovered concealed in a cave. By dusk the Marines in the northern sector had encountered and dealt with only 15 Japanese soldiers, but they had rounded up some 675 Okinawa civilians – mostly old people and children. Even the Kamikazes failed to put in an appearance until dusk. However a few did appear as the light failed and one succeeded in crashing into the battleship *West Virginia*, killing four men and wounding 23. The remainder were either shot down or their pilots decided the time for their supreme sacrifice was not yet opportune.

Further south the force under Rear Admiral Jerrault Wright which carried out the decoy landings on D-Day and 2 April received more attention from the Japanese air force than did the real landings. As dawn was breaking and the ships maneuvered into position for the landings, the Kamikazes arrived and one succeeded in crashing his plane into a tank landing craft with 300 Marines on board. The vessel burst into flames, ammunition exploded and 24 sailors and Marines were killed; 21 others were wounded. Another Kamikaze which smashed into the side of the transport *Hinsale* caused 55 other casualties. The landings did not in fact deceive the Japanese but enabled them to claim on Radio Tokyo that they had 'forced "Jerry" Wright and his men to withdraw . . . after being mowed down one after the other.'

While the landing of stores, equipment and still more men continued unabated, the absence of Japanese soldiers continued to puzzle even the American Intelligence experts. To abandon two valuable airfields without a fight seemed inconceivable. The Japanese must surely be dug in somewhere waiting to give the invaders hell when they came up to their positions. Where were the defenses? Some of the captured civilians who were interrogated said that the Japanese had withdrawn to the east, still others said they had pulled back south. Most of the experts concluded that they were holed up in the rugged terrain of the northern part of Okinawa.

In fact General Ushijima had concentrated his troops in two areas – east and south of the town of Naka, and on the Motobu Peninsula. He had been hoping reinforcements would reach him from Japan before the island was invaded, but even without them he had about 100,000 men, if the Okinawa Home Guard was counted in. This was greatly in excess of American Intelligence estimates. Ushijima had studied the American technique of island invasions, and had seen that in earlier campaigns the forces deployed by the invaders came in overwhelming strength. The old ideas of annihilating the enemy on the beach as the Japanese commanders at Tarawa, Saipan and Iwo Jima had tried to do were no longer valid, and Imperial General Headquarters had laid down a new code of tactics. Ushijima was to allow the enemy to 'land in full' and be 'lured into a position where he cannot receive cover and support from the naval and aerial bombardment . . .

Right: From the second day of the landing US troops began to encounter serious resistance. Okinawan women help to load wounded Americans on to a truck for evacuation.

Below: Supplies are unloaded on 13 April 1945. The development of Okinawa as an American base began soon after L-day, although Japanese resistance lasted for nearly three months.

(and) where the most effective fire power can be brought to bear. His force is then to be wiped out.' Such tactics, the Japanese High Command reckoned, would gain time and inflict maximum casualties; in fact the end was the same – the extermination of the Japanese garrison on Okinawa, and ultimately the defeat of Japan.

Ushijima decided that his best bet for prolonging the defense and inflicting maximum casualties was to abandon the Hagushi beaches and the two airfields. He had originally intended to put both airfields out of commission but the invasion took place before the demolitions his engineers had planned could be put into effect. In the last-minute rush to pull back to the two concentration areas they were abandoned. So far as the Americans were concerned Yontan and Kadena were the most important territorial gains of D-Day. On 2 April the Kadena strip was being used as an emergency landing ground, and next day two strips of the Yontan field could also be used. One of the stories that went the rounds at this time told of a Japanese plane landing on the Yontan airfield on the night of 1/2 April. The pilot taxied up to the filling station, climbed out and asked for fuel in Japanese. A Marine sentry replied and the Emperor lost one pilot.

On 2 and 3 April men of the 7th Infantry Division and Marines of the 1st Marine Division reached the east coast of the island and on 4 April the 1st and 6th Marine Divisions occupied the Katchin Peninsula and a large stretch of the east coast. The operation was now 20 days ahead of the schedule the planners had forecast. Next day the advance was resumed with the Marines moving into the northern half of Okinawa and meeting no serious resistance until they crossed into the Motobu Peninsula.

South of the Bisha River on the second day the GIs of the 96th Division began to encounter increasing resistance in rugged terrain. This resistance, by a rear guard covering the withdrawal of Ushijima's Naha force, was swept aside on 4 April when air reconnaissance flights spotted Japanese troops moving toward Shuri, the ancient capital of Okinawa east of Naha. At long last the aircraft and the battleships had some positive targets, although nobody had yet seen any great concentration of Japanese or pinpointed their defense works. Their real whereabouts was still a mystery. That night however the GIs were subjected for the first time to a heavy artillery bombardment and, although they resumed the advance the next morning, the intensity of the storm of fire that greeted them brought them up short. They had reached the so-called Machinato Line of the Japanese Shuri Zone – an interlocking system of mountain defenses organized in great depth. Here the GIs were destined to remain for the next two weeks.

For the Japanese 3 April was a significant date – it was 'Jimmu Day' – the day

Above: Marine artillerymen hunt for Japanese snipers who have infiltrated their position.
Below: This bulldozer follows close behind advancing Marines and so an infantryman rides shotgun to protect the driver.
Above right: Marines scramble over a stone wall during their advance. Note the flame thrower carried by the man in the center.
Right: Marines raise the Stars and Stripes on Okinawa.

when 2500 years earlier the Emperor Jimmu had initiated a policy of Japanese expansion when he declared that he wished '. . . to make the universe our home.' Jimmu Day was supposed to be a happy occasion and for many years it had always been possible to find some cheerful news in keeping with the spirit of the day. Following the landings on Okinawa, the constant bombing of the home islands and the virtual destruction of Japan's major cities, the Japanese Government had to admit the situation was extremely serious. If Okinawa was lost, Admiral Takahashi pointed out in a broadcast from Radio Tokyo, Japan would be cut off from all the territories she had conquered in the South Pacific. However, there was no need for despair, he said; the Imperial Navy was going to go on the offensive and all would soon be well. In the Japanese Parliament – the Diet – the wizened General Kuniaki Koiso blustered that 'our Japanese heroes' would drive the Americans off Okinawa and then 'retake Saipan and other points.' But the sands were running out for Koiso. In a few days time he was to resign and the aged Admiral Suzuki, charged by the Emperor with the task of finding some honorable way of ending the war, became Premier. Meantime, since the finding of a formula for peace without loss of face would take time and require circumspection and caution to avoid a military coup d'état, there was no question but that Okinawa would be defended vigorously and to the last man.

After the Battle of Leyte Gulf, which saw the beginning of the Kamikaze Corps, the Imperial Japanese Navy had ceased to exist as a practical fighting force. Most of the cruisers had been lost, and the battleships *Yamato*, *Nagato* and *Haruna*, which had limped home, had been bottled up in the Inland Sea. The *Yamato* (863 feet long) and her sister ship the *Musashi* (which had been sunk in October 1944) were the world's biggest battleships. Laid down in 1937 and completed in 1941 they were armed with nine 460mm (18.1-inch) guns capable of hurling a shell of 3200 pounds 42,000 meters (22.5 miles). The *Yamato*'s crew totalled 2800 men.

Shortage of fuel precluded the *Yamato*, *Nagato* and *Haruna* being used for operations. During March, however, an attempt had been made to resuscitate the Second Fleet, by allocating what remained of the dwindling fuel stocks to the *Yamato*, the cruiser *Yakagi* and five destroyers. In an effort to cripple the American invasion fleet off Okinawa Admiral Toyoda, Commander in Chief of the once proud Combined Fleet, decided to use these ships in an operation called 'Ten-Go.' There was little if any coordination between the services as to how the army, navy and air force would act and when. Ten-Go was supposed to be a combined and coordinated triservice operation with mass Kamikaze attacks from the air, Kaiten and other submarines attacking under the sea, and what was left of the Imperial Navy took part. A series of Kaiten and Kamikaze attacks had already been scheduled for 6 April under the code name Kikusui. Literally 'floating chrysanthemum,' Kikusui was the crest of the Kusukoni family. In the fourteenth century Mazashige Kusukoni had led a Japanese army to certain death in a suicide operation. However, Kikusui Operation Number 1 was to be the grand attack which could make the other operations superfluous.

The warships of the reconstituted Second Fleet were commanded by Vice-Admiral Seeichi Ito, who had been Vice-Chief of Naval Operations in 1941 and who was considered to be an outstanding officer. Realizing that desperate circumstances called for desperate action, Ito was willing to accept orders for a suicidal operation without questioning them. He was one of the few senior officers of the Imperial Navy who did. In Tokyo the Naval General Staff were against Toyoda's Kikusui, maintaining that although Japan faced total defeat it was inhuman to order men into an operation of this magnitude which was so uncertain of success. In their view the fleet would never reach Okinawa, so the loss of men and ships was a wasteful sacrifice. Toyoda's own Combined Fleet Headquarters refuted this argument. The loss of Okinawa would be disastrous, they said, and it was the navy's job to cooperate with the army. The fleet might not reach Okinawa but it would attract the attention of a large number of American aircraft. A lull in the land fighting would follow, during which a counterattack by General Ushijima's troops would have considerable chance of success.

Toyoda's order called for the Second Fleet to beach itself in front of the Americans on Okinawa and to fire every gun of every ship until the last shell had been expended or the last ship destroyed. Individual survivors were told that they could join in the land fighting and 'find glory.'

The order was received aboard Ito's flagship, the *Yamato*, during the afternoon of 5 April, as the operation was scheduled for 8 April. Ito promptly summoned his captains to a conference, and there was a storm of protest. Nearly all the commanding officers objected to the operation – not because it meant certain death, but because they considered it meant squandering what was left of the Imperial Navy for a very dubious return. There was no question of Ito's subordinates not being prepared to give their lives, and those of their men, for the Emperor. But they were dominated by a philosophy that had come to them long ago through their association with Britain's Royal Navy: 'Fight bravely, but not in vain.' The conference lasted for five hours, during which some heated comments were passed about the planning capabilities of Combined Fleet Headquarters, safe in its air-raid shelter. But discipline held. When Ito said that the order must be obeyed, the

Above and top: In a vain attempt to open communications with the defenders of Okinawa, the huge battleship *Yamato* sortied from Japan. On 7 April she was sent to the bottom by carrier planes.

argument stopped and the commanders returned to their ships to prepare for the forthcoming action.

On board the ships the return of the captains spelled feverish activity. Bayonets were sharpened ready for the hand-to-hand fighting many of the crews expected to see ashore. Fuel sufficient only for a one way passage was taken on, and the crews were weeded out, only those needed to man the ships remaining. (Among those who were disembarked was a batch of midshipmen, fresh from the Naval Academy, who had arrived only a few days earlier. Many of these young men wished to take part in the operation but they were not permitted to do so.) Finally there were the farewell parties, at which many bottles of sake were consumed. These broke up with the singing of *Doki no Sakura* ('Cherry Blossoms of the same rank') – an old Naval Academy song.

The Second Fleet steamed out of the Inland Sea that night, and by 0600 hours on 6 April it was southwest of Kyushu, heading due south for Okinawa on a zigzag course. If all went well it was scheduled to reach the American landing beaches just before daylight on the 8th. An antisubmarine formation was assumed after the ships passed through the Bungo Strait, and for some hours 20 Zeros of the Fifth Air Fleet provided an aerial umbrella. However, as land receded the Zeros returned, and the reconnaissance seaplanes from the *Yamato* and *Yahagi* were flown off to prevent their destruction in the forthcoming battle. There was no need for reconnaissance; the whereabouts of the Americans was well known – just as the Americans knew of Ito's approach. Five miles behind Ito's fleet the US submarines *Threadfin* and *Hackleback* trailed the fleet and watched in fascination as the monstrous *Yamato* moved across their periscopes. At dawn on 7 April US flying boats arrived to tighten the watch.

Low, heavy clouds provided perfect protection for the attackers when the Americans struck at 1230 hours. Shortly after noon the *Yamato*'s radar had picked up two large formations of planes converging on her, and the first of them appeared overhead even before the message had been relayed to the other ships. There was no question of changing course, but the fleet speeded up to 27 knots, swung into two lines with 5000-yard intervals between ships, and opened fire. From start to finish Ito's fleet stood little chance. Although the *Yamato*'s AA guns put up a formidable curtain of steel, it was of little use. Planes were shot down but new attack waves came on incessantly. This was the fourth time the Americans had attacked the giant battleship and they were determined to sink her on this occasion.

The first bomb struck the *Yamato* at 1240 hours, and 10 minutes later a torpedo found its mark. Thereafter many more bombs and at least 15 torpedoes struck home. Three hours of steady attack finally doomed the great battleship. In all 300 US carrier-based planes struck at Ito's ship. According to Ensign Yoshida who survived the action:

'. . . bombs, bullets and torpedoes reduced the mighty battleship to a state of complete confusion. . . . The desolate decks were reduced to shambles, with nothing but cracked and twisted steel plates remaining. . . . . Big guns were inoperable because of the increasing list, and only a few machine guns were intact. . . . One devastating blast in the emergency dispensary killed all its occupants including the medical officers and corpsmen. . . .'

The ship was listing at an angle of 35 degrees when, shortly after 1400 hours, American Hellcats and Avengers returned to the attack. According to Yoshida:

'. . . the enemy came plunging through the clouds to deliver the coup de grace. . . . It was impossible to evade. . . . I could hear the Captain vainly shouting, "Hold on, men! Hold on, men! . . ." I heard the Executive Officer report to the Captain in a heartbroken voice, "Correction of list hopeless! . . ." Men were jumbled together in disorder on the deck, but a group of staff officers squirmed out of the pile and crawled over to the Commander in Chief for a final conference. Admiral Ito struggled to his feet. His Chief of Staff then arose and saluted. A prolonged silence followed during which they regarded each other solemnly. Ito looked around, shook hands deliberately with his staff officers, and then went resolutely into his cabin. The Captain concerned himself with saving the Emperor's portrait.'

At 1423 hours the ship slid under completely, followed by the blast, rumble and shock of compartments bursting from air pressure and exploding magazines already submerged. By 1500 hours not only *Yamato*, but the *Yahagi* and two destroyers *Asashimo* and *Kamakaze* had all been sunk. Two other destroyers the *Isokaze* and *Kasumi*, dead in the water, were sunk by other Japanese destroyers, after their crews had been rescued. Of the fleet only five destroyers now remained, and they returned to port next day. This greatest of suicide actions which was aborted had cost Japan six out of 10 ships and the lives of more than 2500 men.

After the battle Combined Fleet Headquarters issued a communiqué which read: 'Owing to the brave and sacrificial fighting of the Second Fleet, our Special Attack planes achieved great result.' The truth was that this last desperate fleet sortie of the Imperial Navy had ended in a miserable failure. The once glorious Combined Fleet, which had prided itself on commanding the entire Western Pacific, had been driven ignominiously from the seas around Japan.

4.STALEMATE

Left: Marines smoke out the Japanese defenders from their strongpoint in a cave.
Below left: A heavy machine gun of the US Army's 96th Division fires on Japanese positions, 4 April 1945.
Right: Major General Lemuel Shepherd commanded the 6th Marine Division on Okinawa.
Below: Marines detonate a satchel charge in the entrance of a Japanese cave.

With the rapid advance of the Marines in the northern half and that of the GIs in the south, Ushijima's forces on Okinawa were effectively cut in two. The main part of the Japanese garrison was in the south, and by 8 April the advance toward Shuri and Naha had ground to a halt. The GIs of the 96th Division had driven in the Japanese outposts but they could not pierce the elaborate and carefully prepared defenses of the Machinato Line. The Japanese had made full use of the geological structure of the island – coral-limestone caves occurring naturally as a result of the upward pressure of volcanic forces which had created Okinawa and broken much of its surface into

sharp ridges and ravines. These caves provided splendid defensive positions – particularly to a people with the endless patience of the Japanese. They occurred usually in the faces of cliffs and ridges in defilade from naval gunfire and all but invulnerable from the air. The Machinato Line had been constructed by linking together a series of the caves. They were of course susceptible to manmade improvements, but fortunately on Okinawa there had been little time or materials available for such work. Here were few of the reinforced concrete bulkheads, steel doors and elaborate galleries that had been encountered on Iwo Jima. But many of the natural positions had been developed to obtain scientifically interlocking fields of fire for mutual protection, so it was not possible to bypass the Machinato positions.

The Americans brought up artillery and pounded the Jap positions but the point has been made that many of them were in an acute defilade. Moreover there was an acute shortage of ammunition. On 6 April Kamikaze bombers had sunk two of the three ammunition ships which had just arrived off Okinawa and this probably contributed to the shortage. Bad weather

also hampered the unloading of stores over the beaches between the 4th and 6th and this also added to the problems of the troops.

It was now the turn of the Japanese. Imperial General Headquarters in Tokyo had radioed a 'suggestion' to Ushijima that the time was ripe for a counterattack, and Ushijima duly passed it on to his subordinate commander in Shuri. Four battalions took part and the attack was planned in considerable detail In fact it took practically everything into consideration – except the terrain. As a result of this omission and some hard fighting by the GIs the effort ended in complete frustration.

The attack began at midnight on 12 April when the Japanese left the safety of their caves and advanced toward the entrenched Americans. They had been given a slogan for the occasion: 'Seven lives to repay our country' – meaning, evidently, that each man was supposed to kill seven Americans before going to join his ancestors. In the event they were singularly unsuccessful. Not only did they fail to kill seven for one but when they were driven back in the early hours of the morning they left 200 dead behind them.

Bottom: Phosphorus shells explode on an enemy-held ridge as Marines wait to move in and assault it.
Right: A flame-throwing tank of the 7th Infantry Division attacks a Japanese bunker on Hill 178.
Below: The corpse of a Japanese soldier caught by a flame thrower.

The next night (13 April), however, they tried again. This time the attack began shortly after 2100 hours with a fire fight followed by several assaults in considerable strength, and it flickered intermittently all night. The GIs were well dug in and the Japanese were unable to penetrate their defenses. One feature was notable about this attack. For once the Japanese failed to display the spirit and determination that generally characterized their soldiers. The fact was they were close to exhaustion and their morale was low before the assault started.

The next few days on the southern front were relatively quiet. The Kamikaze attacks on the armada off the island also appeared to have tapered off. To a large extent this was due to the rapid buildup of a land-based air force on Yontan and Kadena. The shipping congestion was also being reduced as men and stores were unloaded, so enabling the transports to disperse to safer waters. Now that the invasion force was well established ashore it was also possible to reduce the numbers of warships, although five battleships, five cruisers and 17 destroyers were retained to back up the fire support now provided by the GIs' and

Marines' own artillery. Every night, until the Japanese on Okinawa were finally silenced, the naval vessels stood by off southern Okinawa to shell or illuminate targets indicated by shore fire-control parties. Star shell proved to be one of the best ways of uncovering Japanese attempts to infiltrate the American lines and this was expended liberally.

As a prelude to its capture the island of Ie-Shima was subjected to a naval bombardment and air attack which lasted until 15 April when Minna-shima, four miles to the south, was occupied and three artillery battalions deployed there to support the main landing. After a heavy naval bombardment and air strike men of the 77th Division landed on the south and southwest coasts of Ie-shima without difficulty, and by the evening its airfield was in American hands. The Japanese garrison of two battalions of infantry supplemented by a large number of civilian 'Home Guard' had wrecked the runways and airfield installations and then retired to elaborately prepared defensive positions on the high ground east of the airfield and north of the town of Ie. Many of the defenses were underground networks of tunnels and caverns burrowed below the ridge of high ground. There were scores of hiding places and every hole in the ground had to be poked into since the Japanese had a habit of lying low and coming to life when least expected. Some of the holes needed treatment with hand grenades and flame-throwers, while others were sealed with demolitions. It was 26 April before the last of the defenders had been accounted for and the GIs suffered 1120 casualties of whom 172 were killed; 4716 Japanese were killed and 149 taken prisoner.

When the 27th Division was landed on 10 April there were approximately 160,000 American troops ashore on Okinawa and yet the situation on both the northern and southern fronts remained more or less the same. Men in the ships, shaken by the repeated Kamikaze attacks, grumbled that the men ashore were 'dragging their feet.' The trouble was the formidable strength of the Japanese defense works, especially on the southern front, and the fact that the GIs and Marines had been trained to conserve their strength – to rely on artillery and air strikes to knock out major obstacles before infantry was committed to an assault. It was a technique which kept the casualty list short, but on Okinawa it meant waiting until heavy artillery was brought ashore and deployed for action.

In the event the northern front was cleared up fairly quickly. Having sealed off the northern end of Okinawa the 6th Marine Division set about clearing the Motobu Peninsula. The Japanese were in position on the 1500-foot high Yae Take hills in the center of the peninsula. These hills dominated the surrounding countryside but they had not the same potential for defense as the coral-limestone caves of the

Above: A mortar crew of the 7th Infantry Division pictured in action against Japanese positions on 19 April 1945.

Below: An eight-inch howitzer of the 749th Field Artillery Battalion fires on Japanese positions. This was that weapon's first use in the Pacific war.

Above: A Marine offers comfort to a comrade who broke down after the death of his buddy.
Above right: Men of the 6th Marine Division advance.

Machinato Line. By 19 April the Marines had driven the Japanese from their positions. From then until the end of the month when they were moved to the southern front they were engaged in mopping up in the north of the island.

At 0640 hours on 19 April three US divisions attacked the Machinato Line. The night before the attack took place the ships providing fire support had deliberately refrained from illuminating the battle zone. This, it was thought, would enable the GIs to deploy for the attack unseen and – in view of the intense bombardment which went on throughout the night – unheard. Every naval gun that could be ranged on the enemy positions was included in the fire plan. Ashore 27 battalions of artillery rained 19,000 shells on the Japanese positions for 40 minutes before the assault, and 650 aircraft added bombs, rockets, napalm and strafing to the general din. The infantry assault then went in, the GIs hoping that if the Japanese had not been blown to smithereens then at the very least they would have been so stunned by the bombardment as to be helpless. The Americans were soon disillusioned. Their advance came to a standstill when Japanese troops – seemingly untouched by the great mass of explosive material that had been showered down on them – emerged from their caves to take up their battle positions. Only on the extreme right was the Machinato Line pierced.

For the next five days bitter fighting continued and the Americans' progress was measured only in yards. The Japanese fought tenaciously, stubbornly contesting every inch of ground. Their positions were bombed from the air, strafed and subjected to tremendous artillery bombardment. Yet they clung to them until the sheer weight of attack penetrated and force them to abandon them and fall back. Then the process was repeated. The battle for Okinawa – essentially an infantry battle despite the weight of artillery and air support that was deployed – was the toughest and most prolonged of any in the Pacific war with the exception of Guadalcanal. It was also distinguished by the fact that naval gunfire was:

'employed longer and in greater quantities in the battle of Okinawa than in any other in history. It supported the ground troops and complemented the artillery from the day of the landing until action moved to the extreme southern tip of the island, where the combat area was so restricted that there was a danger of shelling American troops.'

Night illumination with star shell, usually delivered by destroyers, was also a great help to the troops, thwarting Japanese tactics of infiltration and night attack. The US Army historians wrote in *Okinawa: The Land Battle*:

'Time and time again naval night illumination caught Japanese troops forming or advancing for counterattacks and infiltration, and made it possible for the automatic weapons and mortars of the infantry to turn back such groups. It was very difficult for the Japanese to stage a night counterattack of any size without being detected.'

5. MORE KAMIKAZES

The major phase of Kikusui Operation No 1 had achieved nothing, but the subsidiary operations which continued throughout April, May and June scored some minor successes. Ohnishi's planes came down from Kyushu and 1465 Kamikaze planes took part in day and night attacks on targets at Okinawa. These attacks accounted for the heaviest of all Kamikaze-inflicted damage. According to the official report of the Commander in Chief US Pacific Fleet 26 American ships were sunk, and 164 damaged by suicide attacks between 6 April and 22 June. This figure included the victims of sporadic small-scale suicide efforts which occupied another 200 Japanese army and navy planes.

During April the Ohkas scored their first hit. After the Ohka sortie of 21 March had ended so ignominiously, there was some hesitation about selecting the right moment and proper conditions for using this weapon again. The opportunity presented itself on 12 April when Ohka sorties were ordered as part of Kikusui Operation No 2. Eight Ohkas participated in an attack during the morning, along with 80 Kamikaze planes and more than 100 escort fighters. They headed for Okinawa by varying courses to converge on the island from different directions. The bombers carrying them also flew low, in order to take advantage of the high cliffs which surrounded the American anchorages off the island.

Of the eight mother planes in this attack, six were shot down after making their release and only one returned to base to relate the dramatic story of how the pilot of one Ohka, Lieutenant Saburo Dolii, had performed his mission. Dolii, 22 years old, appears to have been a placid and somewhat taciturn individual. During the flight out to Okinawa he slept on a pile of sacks in the back of the Betty bomber. Wakened as they approached the target area, he shook hands with the crew before climbing through the bomb bay into his tiny rocket-powered craft. A battleship was selected as his objective and he was released 20,000 yards from his target at an altitude of about 7000 feet. Last seen by the crew of the bomber as it turned west for safety, Dolii was plummeting down toward the American ships surrounding his battleship. Later, they said, a column of black smoke could

be seen belching from the general location of the target. Whether Dolii hit a US ship, or whether the damage should be attributed to one of the other Ohka pilots will never be known, but that day the destroyer *Mannert L Abele* was sunk and the destroyer *Stanley* damaged by piloted 'Baka bombs,' as the Americans called the Ohkas.

This operation proved the worth of the Ohka to the Japanese and after this the piloted bombs were used regularly. All in all a total of 74 Ohka missions were dispatched before the war came to an end. Of these 56 were either released from their carrier planes, or shot down while still attached to them. While many Ohka dives were reported as successful, confirmation was questionable. After the war the Americans estimated that only four ever hit a target, and claimed that the weapon was a fiasco. 'It failed,' wrote Admiral J J Clark, 'because it was a one shot mission – the pilots never got any practice!' Yet, even if the Ohka failed to do much material damage, there can be little doubt that the appearance of piloted suicide bombs had a telling effect on the morale of the American sailors.

The Ohka bomb attacks were, of course, supplementary to what might be termed the more 'conventional' Kamikaze strikes. These scored other successes on 12 April. Two fell on the destroyer minelayer *Lindsey*, and although she managed to stay afloat she lost 56 men killed and 51 wounded. The destroyer *Zellars*, the minesweeper *Gladiator* and the antisubmarine patrol vessel *Rall* also suffered extensive damage and casualties.

During the afternoon the Kamikazes set their sights on the battleship *Tennessee* and a formation of Kamikazes made a determined effort to knock out Admiral Deyo's flagship. The first was shot down at a range of 4000 yards; three others were destroyed at a distance of between 500 and 100 yards from the ship, a fifth which was seen to be on fire plunged into the sea close to the vessel's bows. Possibly this Kamikaze was intended as a decoy to distract the *Tennessee*'s crew from the one that really meant business, for at the same time another was seen heading directly for the battleship's bridge. All the antiaircraft guns concentrated on this fresh menace and one of the Kamikaze aircraft's wheels was shot off; this upset the plane's balance

and slightly deflected its course. Missing the bridge it crashed onto one of the antiaircraft guns and slithered along the deck scattering flaming gasoline until it was brought to a shuddering halt when it hit one of the ship's 14-inch gun turrets. The blazing fuel caused the deaths of many of the gunners and the Kamikaze's 250-pound bomb went through the deck to explode and created fires in the interior of the ship. One sailor, blown into the air, landed on top of one of the big gun turrets where he calmly stripped off his burning gasoline-soaked clothes while waiting for someone to turn a fire hose on him. Another sailor, trying to dodge the plane as it slithered across the deck, tripped and fell overboard. When he came to the surface he found himself near burning pieces of the plane. Diving to avoid the flames he came up close to a life raft. Climbing on to it he found he had company – the decapitated body of the Japanese Kamikaze pilot which had been tossed into it by the explosion. In this grisly company the sailor remained for several hours until he was picked up by a destroyer.

When the damage was totted up it was found that although the *Tennessee* had suffered little damage her casualties totalled 23 killed and 106 wounded – of whom 33 were horribly burned. All the crew of the gun on which the Kamikaze first crashed were among the casualties. However, the battleship was still capable of continuing her support mission and she was not withdrawn.

At least three other ships were hit or suffered casualties from near misses on 12 April. The next two days were relatively quiet but the Kamikazes returned with a vengeance on the 16th. That day all hell broke loose when the Japanese launched another Kikusui attack with 220 planes. The destroyers on radar picket duty and the minesweepers – isolated and away from the main force – bore the brunt; one destroyer, the *Pringle*, was sunk, while three other destroyers and two minesweepers were badly damaged. One of the ships concerned was the *Laffey*, whose radar operator spotted 50 aircraft closing in on her at 0827 hours. Some of these were shot down or driven off by planes of the air umbrella over the invasion fleet before they were within range of the *Laffey*'s guns. However, within the space of 80

Left and above: On 11 May 1945 a Kamikaze crashed through the flight deck of USS *Bunker Hill* resulting in nearly 400 deaths before the fires were controlled.
Below: Not all kamikazes reached their target. A Japanese aircraft explodes over the carrier USS *Bennington*. In the foreground are USS *Hornet's* Hellcats.

minutes the ship was attacked from all sides by 22 aircraft. Although all but one of the attackers were destroyed, she was hit by four bombs and six Kamikazes crashed on her decks. Despite this the *Laffey* remained afloat, and was towed back to the Kerama Retto where she was patched up; six days later she was able to sail to Guam under her own steam but was out of action for the rest of the war. American casualties amounted to 31 killed and 72 wounded, and the cost to the Japanese was at least 21 aircraft.

By the middle of April 1944 there could be little doubt that the Kamikazes were spreading flaming terror as well as scorching burns and searing deaths. The crews of the vessels off Okinawa had shown tremendous courage and fighting spirit. Nevertheless the attacks were causing considerable alarm and despondency; casualties and losses in ships were heavy and there seemed to be no real answer to Kamikaze tactics. Admiral Nimitz therefore once again called for the Superfortress B-29s of the Strategic Air Command to bomb the Japanese airfields in southern Japan from which the Kamikazes were operating. Thus it was that from 17 April

to the middle of May three-quarters of all the available Superfortresses were diverted from bombing industrial targets and Japanese cities to supporting the Okinawa campaign. Over 2000 B-29 sorties were flown against 17 airfields during which 24 of the Superfortresses were lost and 233 damaged, but it was reckoned that they had destroyed 134 Japanese aircraft. This offensive diminished but did not stop the mass attacks on the ships around Okinawa. However, by 11 May there were then sufficient US aircraft operating from the airfields on Okinawa and Ie-Shima, and Admiral Nimitz told Strategic Air Command that the Superfortresses were no longer needed to support the Okinawa operations.

Back in Japan at this time the respective Imperial Navy and Japanese Army High Commands were arguing about the conduct of the war. The Navy saw the Okinawa operations as the decisive battle and wanted to devote their entire resources to it, while the Army, realizing that Okinawa could not be held, wanted to keep as many aircraft as possible for repelling the inevitable attack on the Japanese mainland. In the event a form of compromise was agreed – with Admiral Toyoda withdrawing (on 17 April)

the Tenth Air Fleet with about half the total number of aircraft deployed for the Okinawa operation. This left the Fifth and Third Air Fleets with about 600 aircraft to continue the battle for Okinawa. These were the planes used in the attacks between 6 April and 22 June which took such a heavy toll of the fast carrier force and the shipping around Okinawa.

One of these attacks, toward the end of May, included a new feature: a number of twin-engined bombers, each with 14 Japanese aboard were detailed to land on the Yontan airfield and do as much damage as possible. Four of these raiders were brought down by antiaircraft fire before they reached the airfield, but a fifth made a belly landing and, before its crew was disposed of, seven American planes had been destroyed and 26 others damaged, and two dumps containing 70,000 gallons of aviation fuel had been set on fire.

The last two mass Kamikaze attacks took place in June as the Okinawa campaign was drawing to a close. Meantime the Kaiten operations had been stepped up although they were in fact no more successful than the flamboyant lemming-like self-destruction of the Second Fleet. After the

ill-conceived *Tatara* operation the *I-58* was ordered to support the Second Fleet action with Kaiten attacks on the US ships lured out by the *Yamato*. Spotted by American aircraft she never got near any of the American capital ships. Harried and chased day and night by destroyers and aircraft, its captain eventually called off the operations and returned to port with his Kaiten intact.

I-58 was lucky to get back to Japan. Eight other Japanese submarines were sunk during April and, with the Sixth Fleet's Kaiten carriers reduced to four, a heated argument developed on how the 'Heaven-shakers' should be employed in future operations. The Naval General Staff in Tokyo, and Combined Fleet Head-

quarters, still believed that the best way was against American fleets and fleet bases. Commander Tennosuke Torisu, the torpedo expert on the staff of the Sixth Fleet Headquarters, argued fiercely against this. He claimed that Kaiten should be sent well out to sea to disrupt the Americans' lines of communications. Eventually Tokyo agreed to let two submarines make attacks on supply lines. Their performance would be evaluated and a final decision would be taken on how the Kaiten would operate in the future.

I-47 and *I-36* were selected for the experiment, and they sallied forth on 20 and 23 April respectively. Each was carrying six Kaiten. *I-47* headed for an area through which US ships bound for Okin-

awa from Ulithi would have to pass, while *I-36* made for a similar interception zone between Okinawa and Saipan. *I-36* drew the first blood. Soon after dawn on 27 April she ran into a convoy of 30 ships bound for Okinawa. At 8000 yards distance orders were given for all six Kaiten to be fired. Four got away, but two were jammed in their racks. Ten minutes later four successive explosions shook the submarine. That night a report was radioed to Tokyo claiming 'four victims,' 'estimated to be transports or cargo ships.' Coming when it did, this success seemed an appropriate sacrifice to the Emperor, whose birthday was on 29 April. In fact only one vessel was sunk, the SS *Canada Victory*, so it must be assumed that all four Kaiten pilots had aimed for the same ship.

During the night of 1 May, *I-47*'s captain, Commander Orita, also encountered a convoy. Because the Kaiten were virtually blind in the dark, he decided to attack with conventional torpedoes. Twelve hours later, however, an opportunity came to use the suicide weapons and two Kaiten (Lieutenant Kakizake and Petty Officer Yamaguchi) were fired at targets reported to be a transport escorted by a destroyer. When two explosions were heard in quick succession it was assumed that both targets had been hit. When Orita raised his periscope he could see a destroyer about three miles away. Another Kaiten was launched and a long-delayed explosion eventually suggested that Petty Officer Furukawa had gone to Yasukuni. Four days later two of the three remaining Kaiten, Lieutenant Maeda and Petty Officer Shinkai, were fired at a 'cruiser.' Orita's intention had been to fire all three, but when the telephone link to the last Kaiten broke down, Petty Officer Yokota lived to tell the tale. 'To live, at times, is much more difficult than to die. . . . A lot of patience is required to wait until the best possible moment for dying comes.' These words were used by Orita as consolation when Yokota protested at being deprived of the opportunity to give his life.

I-47 now followed *I-36* back to Japan. After their return a conference in Tokyo concluded that the success of the two most recent sorties justified Commander Torisu's views. Submarine operations would now be left entirely in the hands of the Sixth Fleet Headquarters. Admiral Nagai promptly ordered every available I Class submarine, a total of nine, to be dispatched on Kaiten operations in the western Pacific. By mid-July six had been sunk, but the Japanese claimed that the Kaitens sank 15 tankers and transports, two cruisers, five destroyers, one seaplane tender and six unidentified ships in the last three months of the war. These figures were subsequently declared by the Allies to be spurious. Eighty Kaiten pilots were killed in action, and even if they had sent down 80 ships it is doubtful whether they could have changed the outcome of the land battle for Okinawa.

Left: The night sky is crisscrossed with tracers during a Japanese air raid on Yontan airfield. In the foreground F4U Corsairs are parked.
Bottom: The remains of two transport aircraft destroyed on Yontan.

The raiders were flown in by Mitsubishi Ki-21s on 24 May.
Below: The charred remains of one of the Japanese commandos killed during the raid on Yontan airfield.

6.CLIMAX

By 23 April the GIs of General Hodge's XXIV Corps had battered their way through the Machinato Line at several points and General Ushijima, fearing that the weakened line would break, withdrew to a second and even stronger one covering Shuri. This line extended from the southwestern end of the Machinato airstrip through Maeda and Kochi to Gaja.

There was now a brief pause while both sides regrouped and prepared for the next round. On 30 April the Americans brought up the 1st Marine Division to relieve the 27th Division and 77th Division to take over from the hard-pressed 96th Division. On their side the Japanese brought their 24th Division into action for the first time. The stage was now set, with both sides in contact along the new Japanese defense line.

At dawn on 4 May General Ushijima hurled the fresh 24th Division supported by tanks and artillery against the center of the American line – held by the US 7th Division. A second minor attack, launched simultaneously, hit the 1st Marine Division on the western flank. At the same time squads of Japanese engineers were landed on the west and east coasts behind the American forward troops to disrupt communications. It was an all-out offensive which Ushijima hoped would inflict a

Right: Bazookas support an infantry attack on a ridge two miles north of Naha, the capital of Okinawa.
Below right: Infantrymen follow a tank into an attack on Japanese caves and pillboxes on 6 May.
Below: A flame-throwing tank of the 713th Tank Battalion goes into action on Coral Ridge.

major defeat on the American invaders. According to plan it was to be supported by Kikusui mass attack No 5 from Kyushu, with the Japanese Navy alone contributing 280 planes, and although only 115 aircraft were actually committed they did a lot of damage. As in other such attacks the isolated vessels on radar picket bore the brunt and two destroyers and two tank landing ships were sunk. Moreover, other Kamikaze 'floating chrysanthemums' which broke through the picket line crashed themselves into several other ships in the bay.

Ashore however the engineer commando raids failed completely, the raiders being wiped out, and the 24th Division's attack soon broke down. Caught by American artillery and strike aircraft supplemented by naval gunfire, the Japanese infantry could make no progress. They tried again that night (4/5 May) but their efforts were equally unsuccessful. The offensive cost Ushijima some 5000 men and many guns, for these had been dragged out of their emplacements and caves into the open; other hidden Japanese artillery positions had also been disclosed in the attack. For the Japanese all this amounted to a serious setback and Ushijima now clearly recognized the writing on the wall. So too did the Japanese High Command in Tokyo who judged that the launching of the offensive had been a serious mistake since it greatly diminished the length of time that the Japanese garrison on Okinawa could hold out. After it units had to be amalgamated and reorganized with men doing administrative duties being posted to fighting units; ammunition expenditure also had to be rationed.

Ushijima's offensive more or less coincided with the transfer of the 6th Marine Division from the northern part of Okinawa to the southern front. The Marines had completed their mission of mopping up the Motobu Peninsula, and General Buckner, the Tenth Army commander, was anxious to resume the offensive and destroy what was left of Ushijima's forces. With the 77th Division and the 1st and 6th Marine Divisions still in hand Buckner was faced with a dilemma: he could either launch a frontal attack in the hope that the sheer weight of the assault would smash through the Japanese defenses; alternatively he could try to envelop Ushijima's force by amphibious landings on the southern tip of the island behind the Japanese. In the event Buckner decided on a frontal attack – two attacks in fact, one on each flank – and his forces were organized into two corps, with the Marines (6th and 1st Divisions) on the right and the 77th and 96th Divisions on the left. (The 6th and 1st Marine Divisions constituted the Marine III Amphibious Corps; the 77th and 96th Divisions formed the XXIV Corps.) To back up the attack the five support ships were also divided into two groups, one stationed off the Hagushi beaches and one in Nakagusuku Wan.

For a week there was a lull in the fighting – broken on the 8th when the news of Germany's unconditional surrender was flashed to Okinawa. Turner reported:

'It was the most quiet day yet experienced by our forces in this area. Many ships conducted Divine Services in Thanksgiving for Victory in Europe. At exactly 1200 hours one round from every gun ashore accompanied a full gun salvo from every possible fire support ship directed at the enemy, as a complimentary and congratulatory gesture to our Armed Forces in Europe.'

Three days later in appalling weather General Simon Bolivar Buckner launched his offensive. Torrential rain turned the country, except for the rocky outcrops, into a sea of mud. Tanks bogged down, wheeled transport could not move at all and even amphibious tractors were often useless. In consequence the Americans had to carry up all their supplies and bring back their wounded. To add to this the Japanese resisted bitterly. However, both flanks of the Japanese line were finally pierced and on 21 May Buckner's men reached the outskirts of Shuri. The line of defenses covering the town still held, but American pressure was so great that Ushijima judged

Far left: A party of Marines strings up communications lines behind advancing troops.
Above left: An M-18 of the 77th Division's 306th Antitank Company fires into enemy lines.
Left: A caterpillar tractor pulls a Marine ambulance jeep out of the mud which made roads almost impassable during the rainy season.

54

that his troops would not be able to hold the line much longer. Casualties had reduced the two divisions and mixed brigade which had originally been deployed on the southern front, to about a third of their strength, and so the Japanese commander decided to withdraw to a ridge which, with its caves, dugouts and tunnels gave his force a better chance of prolonging resistance on the island. By the end of the month the Japanese had completed their withdrawal and the Americans occupied the shattered town of Shuri on 31 May. Ushijima's depleted army was now in a sorry state; its strength was down to about 30,000 men of whom only a third were fighting troops, most of its artillery had been lost, there were insufficient rifles and machine guns to go round, a paucity of ammunition and there was a critical shortage of food. The end could not long be delayed.

There was fierce fighting early in June but by the 12th the Americans had gained control of the ridge and driven off a counter-attack by Ushijima's last reserve. The Japanese fought on but as their account of the battle says:

'By the 17th organized resistance was no longer possible and nothing remained but to fight it out around the caves, rocky crags and broken ground at the southern tip of the island. Individual fighting of a desperate nature continued for a while with rifles, grenades and swords but, against enemy superiority, particularly in flame-throwing tanks, human beings were helpless.'

Realizing that resistance was no longer possible, Ushijima ordered the remnants of his army to disperse and individuals to travel north and to form guerrilla bands.

The struggle for Okinawa was almost over, yet General Buckner did not live to see the end. On 18 June an observation post to which he had gone to watch an attack by the 8th Marine Regiment came under fire from one of the few remaining Japanese guns. In the bombardment one of

Bottom: Marines cover the tower of a Christian church, which provided a vantage point for Japanese snipers.
Below: Lieutenant Colonel Richard Ross attaches the Stars and Stripes to a Japanese flagpole, after the 5th Marine Regiment captured Shuri castle in May 1945.

the shells hurled a block of coral at the American commander. Mortally wounded, he died within a few minutes, a scant two miles and four days short of his goal, the capture of the island.

When the Americans stormed ashore on Okinawa they had expected an immediate and vicious response from the garrison. To everybody's surprise the defenders offered little resistance, and the landing beaches were secured in the face of only a mild defense. Not until the American troops started to move inland was the pattern of previous assaults repeated. Then the Americans experienced another version of the storming of Iwo Jima. The defenders fought desperately, inflicting heavy casualties on the invaders. Gradually they were pushed back to the hills in the southern part of the island. By VE Day, 8 May, the Japanese were beaten.

In the next three weeks General Ushijima managed to perform a minor miracle by organizing another line of defense, but he knew the end was close. By this time the

Above left: After their surrender, three Japanese soldiers carry a wounded comrade from their cave.
Left: The funeral of Lieutenant General Simon Bolivar Buckner, commander of the US Tenth Army, who was killed in action by shellfire on 18 June.
Below: The bodies of Japanese defenders lie in the ruins of Shuri castle after its capture.

Japanese troops knew it also. Bombarded by millions of leaflets which assured them of fair treatment, a few considered surrendering. Most decided against it and committed suicide instead.

Admiral Ota's naval force made a final Banzai charge on 13 June against the forces which had landed in the vicinity of Oroku. Nothing more is known of Ota and his men. The last message received from him was sent on 6 June:

'More than two months have passed since we engaged the invaders. In complete unity and harmony with the army, we have made every effort to crush the enemy.

... I tender herewith my deepest apology to the Emperor for my failure to better defend the Empire, the grave task with which I was entrusted.

The troops under my command have fought gallantly, in the finest tradition of the Japanese navy. Fierce bombing and bombardments may deform the mountains of Okinawa but cannot alter the loyal spirit of our men. We hope and pray for the perpetuation of the Empire and gladly give our lives for that goal.

To the Navy Minister and all my superior officers I tender my sincerest appreciation and gratitude for their kindness of many years. At the same time, I earnestly beg you to give thoughtful consideration to the families of my men who fall at this outpost as soldiers of the Emperor.

With my officers and men I give three cheers for the Emperor and pray for the everlasting peace of the Empire.

Though my body decay in remote Okinawa, my spirit will persist in defense of the homeland.

Minoru Ota
Naval Commander'

Before he perished Ota is known to have issued one order which typifies the suicidal attitude of his kind. A huge cave inside the Japanese lines was serving as a field hospital and 300 badly wounded Japanese Marines of Ota's detachment lay there. Fearing that the Americans would flush out the cave with flame throwers before asking questions, Ota ordered the senior medical officer to make sure the patients had an honorable death without any further suffering. The doctor and his orderlies walked along the long rows of sick men and methodically squeezed hypodermic syringes into 300 outstretched arms.

No one appears to know quite what happened to Tanamachi's 7000 airmen. Like many of the army units they probably fought on until they were annihilated. That at least was what happened to one isolated detachment whose commanding officer reported in a final message:

'My men are in high spirits and fighting gallantly. We pray for the final victory of the motherland. We will fight to the last man in defense of this outpost. . . .'

Above: Marines cross into Naha over a footbridge thrown across the river by American engineers.
Top left: A bazooka pictured in action from the shelter of a tomb.
Left: A patrol from the 6th Marine Division searches the streets of Naha, Okinawa's capital.
Top: Engineers scan a roadway with a mine detector in June 1945.

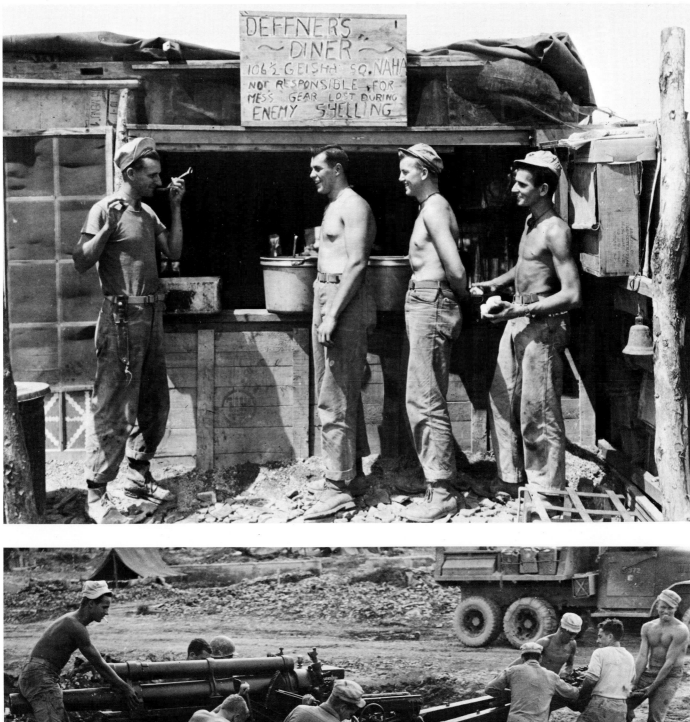

Left: A Marine 'chow line' near Naha.
Below left: Marine artillerymen manhandle a 105mm howitzer into position on 9 June.
Right: Japanese naval troops surrender to the Americans.
Bottom: Japanese are flushed out of a cane field.
Below: Men of the 15th Marine Regiment move into the outskirts of Naha on 6 June 1945.

Inside the cave which sheltered his headquarters, General Ushijima relaxed with a bottle of whiskey while he listened to the reports coming from his scattered units. His last defense line had disintegrated and the Japanese troops had become a disorganized rabble, skulking in holes, hungry and without hope. Ushijima was a realist and he knew that it was finished. Quietly he dictated a farewell message to Tokyo:

'To my great regret we are no longer able to continue the fight. For this failure I tender deepest apologies to the Emperor and the people of the homeland. We will make one final charge to kill as many of the enemy as possible. I pray for the souls of men killed in battle and for the prosperity of the Imperial Family.

Death will not quell the desire of my spirit to defend the homeland.

With deepest appreciation of the kindness and cooperation of my superiors and my colleagues in arms, I bid farewell to all of you forever.'

A poetic postscript to his letter read:

'Green grass dies in the islands without waiting for fall,
But it will be reborn verdant in the springtime of the homeland.
Weapons exhausted, our blood will bathe the earth, but the spirit will survive,
Our spirits will return to protect the motherland.'

In the early morning of 22 June, Ushijima and his chief of staff, General Isama Cho, dressed themselves in their best

Right: A US Navy Grumman Avenger commences its bombing run on a target on Okinawa, June 1945.
Below: Infantrymen of the 7th Division take cover during the final stages of the fighting on Okinawa, 18 June 1945.

uniforms and pinned their medals to their tunics. A quilt had been laid out on a narrow ledge of rock just outside the cave. Over it was a white sheet symbolizing death. The two generals knelt. According to the Samurai code hari-kiri is supposed to be committed facing toward the Imperial Palace in Tokyo. Because of the narrowness of the ledge Ushijima and Cho had to face west to the Pacific. A staff officer handed the two generals each a knife. Then came *seppuku* – the slash across the abdomen. Behind Ushijima another officer raised his sword and quickly struck off Ushijima's head. Cho was decapitated in the same way a few moments later.

The battle for Okinawa was over, but not the dying, since Ushijima's example was followed by the most grotesque series of suicides. Naked Japanese soldiers would dash out of their caves, hurl rocks at the Americans and then race back behind the rocks and slit their throats or blow themselves up with grenades. A particularly bizarre incident occurred when a patrol of US Marines suddenly found themselves in a clearing surrounded by a strong force of Japanese accompanied by a number of women. With unusual presence of mind, the patrol commander smiled, pulled out his cigarettes and offered them around. A few of the Japanese soldiers dropped their weapons and reached for the cigarettes. Their officers not only refused but turned away. Then one drove his sword straight through his woman companion, handed his sword and wristwatch to one of the Americans, stepped back and blew off his head with a grenade. This infected the others who promptly killed the other women and then committed suicide. For two hours the US patrol was compelled to watch a suicidal blood bath.

In the fighting for Okinawa Japanese casualties amounted to more than 100,000 killed. Of these deaths at least half were incurred in suicidal operations. Strategically the Americans had won a great victory, for they were now on Japan's very doorstep. Their losses were also high – more than 12,500 killed and missing, twice the casualty rate of Iwo Jima.

Okinawa was now to become the final base for the invasion of Japan.

7. EPILOGUE

The Okinawa campaign has been compared to that of Iwo Jima. In fact the comparison is incorrect and unfair to the gallant US Marines who secured Iwo Jima at a terrible cost to themselves. The Okinawa terrain had none of the natural defensive qualities of Iwo Jima; the Japanese had no previously prepared defenses between Yontan and Shuri. Only the incredible fanaticism of the Japanese soldier held the line, and that fanaticism for almost two months was sufficient against an invader who held absolute command of the air, who had the equivalent

Below: The official Japanese surrender ceremony on Okinawa.

of two armored divisions, who, to an overwhelming strength in artillery, had added the stupendous power of the guns of a great fleet, and who had an almost unlimited superiority in men, equipment and supplies.

It is always easy to be wise after the event and to oversimplify the problems facing a commander. Any serious student of war will question the wisdom of General Buckner's decision to launch a frontal attack at the beginning of May rather than try to break the deadlock by landing more Marines in the rear of the Japanese – as the Marines themselves suggested. No doubt Buckner saw the situation as analogous to that in Italy in 1943, and considered that

the proposed Marine amphibious landing, like the Anzio operation, would have been beyond range of support from the main front. Against this it can be argued that he had the finest body of amphibious troops in the Pacific and Buckner's critics believe that his decision to opt for a frontal attack was an error of overcaution.

In the event Buckner's strategy worked, but at a heavy price in men. Moreover, instead of the 40 days estimated by the original planners, the Okinawa campaign took 82. On the other hand the tactical handling of the US Fifth Fleet – the armada which carried the assault force to Okinawa and set it down there so successfully – was

nothing short of brilliant. The logistical support of the great fleet at sea over a protracted period was unprecedented, and a most remarkable demonstration of efficiency.

The object of the Okinawa campaign was to secure a base for the invasion of Japan. It succeeded in doing far more than this, for the campaign cost Japan the remainder of her effective navy. Apart from the loss of the *Yamato*, sunk in the abortive sortie against the invasion force, innumerable minor vessels were sunk, and by mid-June the once proud Imperial Japanese Navy had ceased to exist as a fighting force.

The same was true of the Japanese air force. Coupled with the toll taken of Japanese aircraft in the Philippines and during the Iwo Jima campaign, the numbers destroyed in the covering operations for Okinawa crippled the striking power and the defensive power of that part of the Japanese air force which was to protect the home islands. Only the suicide tactics of the Kamikaze organization kept Japanese airmen in the picture and even that by the end of the Okinawa campaign was becoming a diminishing asset. Although the Japanese military forces involved were not large in relation to the actual size of the Japanese armies, the loss in military prestige and in material was considerable.

Meanwhile the tremendous achievement of American production was now beginning to play its full part in the war against Japan. The material losses of the campaign – and of the operations to secure Iwo Jima and recapture the Philippines – were quickly made up. By the end of Okinawa the Philippines were already a vast base for the invasion of Japan. Even while the fighting was continuing, the work of preparing Okinawa for its eventual role as a staging area for the invasion was well under way.

The military operations that followed the capture of Okinawa were small and unimportant. They consisted of the seizure and consolidation of other small islands in the Ryukyus. The vital factor in this period was the 'buildup' and that proceeded unhampered by the Japanese – swiftly and inexorably.

The three campaigns – to liberate the Philippines, capture Iwo Jima and Okinawa – were in combination the greatest successes in the great successes of the Pacific war. With the earlier capture of the Marianas they made possible, first, the wiping out by incendiary bombing of the great cities of Japan and second the provision of all that was necessary for the staging of the eventual descent on the Japanese mainland. They, and not the atomic bomb, were the decisive factor in the subsequent Japanese surrender.

APPENDIX

The Kikusui (floating chrysanthemum) operations

In addition to a number of minor raids by up to 20 planes on 'off' days the Japanese launched 10 major Kamikaze attacks on the US armada off Okinawa. These are detailed in the following table.

Attack No	Date	Navy	Army	Total
1 (TEN-GO)	6– 7 April (1945)	230	125	355
2	12–13 April	125	60	185
3	15–16 April	120	45	165
4	27–28 April	65	50	115
5	3– 4 May	75	50	125
6	10–11 May	70	80	150
7	23–25 May	65	100	165
8	27–29 May	60	50	110
9	3– 7 June	20	30	50
10	21–22 June	30	15	45
	Total	860	605	1465

Number of Aircraft* — Navy, Army, Total

* These figures do NOT include the aircraft which escorted the Kamikazes to the battle zone.

Together with individual Kamikaze attacks not listed in the table it is estimated that approximately 1900 suicide sorties were made against the US naval forces during the Okinawa campaign. Apart from these there were hundreds of attacks by conventional dive bombers and torpedo bombers.

INDEX

Acknowledgments

The author would like to thank
Jane Laslett, the editor
Adrian Hodgkins, the designer
Anthony Robinson for writing the captions
Penny Murphy for preparing the index
Richard Natkiel for supplying the maps

Picture Credits

The author would also like to thank the individuals
and agencies listed below for the use of their
photographs
Robert Hunt: pp 16, 27
Imperial War Museum: pp 14 (bottom), 17 top left,
25, 42–3
National Archives: pp 12 (top), 12 (bottom), 13, 14–5,
17 (top right), 18 (top), 18–9 (bottom), 33 (bottom),
34–5, 37 (bottom), 38 (top), 38 (bottom), 40 (top),
47 (top right), 47 (top left), 47 (bottom), 55 (bottom),
62 (top)
US Army: pp 7 (top), 23, 35 (top), 40 (bottom)
42 (top), 43 (top), 44 (top and bottom), 49 (top), 50,
53 (top), 55 (center), 60 (bottom), 61 (top), 62 (bottom)
US Coast Guard: pp 4–5, 8 (top)
US Marine Corps: pp 1, 8–9 (bottom), 9 (top),
19 (top), 30 (top), 30–1 (bottom), 31 (top), 33 (top),
36 (top), 36 (bottom), 37 (top), 41 (top and bottom),
45 (top left), 45 (top right), 48, 49 (bottom), 51 (top
and bottom), 52, 53 (center), 54 (top and bottom),
55 (top), 56 (top and bottom), 57 (top and bottom),
58 (top and bottom), 59 (all three), 60 (top)
US Navy: pp 2–3, 6 (top and bottom), 7 (bottom),
10 (all), 14 (top), 17 (bottom), 24, 26–7, 28 (top and
bottom), 29, 32 (top and bottom)